The Greeks and Hedging Explained

Financial Engineering Explained

About the series

Financial Engineering Explained is a series of concise, practical guides to modern finance, focusing on key, technical areas of risk management and asset pricing. Written for practitioners, researchers and students, the series discusses a range of topics in a non-mathematical but highly intuitive way. Each self-contained volume is dedicated to a specific topic and offers a thorough introduction with all the necessary depth, but without too much technical ballast. Where applicable, theory is illustrated with real world examples, with special attention to the numerical implementation.

Series Editor:
Wim Schoutens, Department of Mathematics, Catholic University of Leuven.

Series Advisory Board:
Peter Carr, Executive Director, NYU Mathematical Finance; Global Head of Market Modeling, Morgan Stanley.
Ernst Eberlein, Department of Mathematical Stochastics, University of Freiburg.
Matthias Scherer, Chair of Mathematical Finance, Technische Universität München.

Titles in the series:
Equity Derivatives Explained, Mohamed Bouzoubaa
The Greeks and Hedging Explained, Peter Leoni

Forthcoming titles:
Smile Pricing Explained, Peter Austing
Interest Rates Explained Volume 1, Jörg Kienitz
Interest Rates Explained Volume 2, Jörg Kienitz
Dependence Modeling Explained, Matthias Scherer and Jan-Frederik Mai

Submissions: Wim Schoutens – wim@schoutens.be

Financial Engineering Explained series
Series Standing Order ISBN: 978–1137–32733–8

You can receive future titles in this series as they are published by placing a standing order. Please contact your bookseller or, in case of difficulty, write to us at the address below with your name and address, the title of the series and the ISBN quoted above.

Customer Services Department, Macmillan Distribution Ltd, Houndmills, Basingstoke, Hampshire RG21 6XS, England

---

The Greeks and Hedging Explained

Peter Leoni

KU Leuven, Belgium

First published 2014 by
PALGRAVE MACMILLAN

Palgrave Macmillan in the UK is an imprint of Macmillan Publishers Limited, registered in England, company number 785998, of Houndmills, Basingstoke, Hampshire RG21 6XS.

Palgrave Macmillan in the US is a division of St Martin's Press LLC, 175 Fifth Avenue, New York, NY 10010.

Palgrave Macmillan is the global academic imprint of the above companies and has companies and representatives throughout the world.

Palgrave® and Macmillan® are registered trademarks in the United States, the United Kingdom, Europe and other countries

ISBN 978-1-137-35073-2   ISBN 978-1-137-35074-9 (eBook)
DOI 10.1057/9781137350749

A catalogue record for this book is available from the British Library.

A catalog record for this book is available from the Library of Congress.

Contents

List of Figures

Preface

F.A.Q.

Q: What do hedging and Greeks have in common?
A: Derivatives traders have developed their own language over time and 'Greeks' refer to particular exposures a trading book with options has. Managing or hedging your Greeks is what you have to learn before you can get to trading.

Q: So this book is about trading?
A: Actually it sheds a light on derivatives and options in particular. It focuses on the options world and the dynamics rather than listing trading strategies. But successful traders are good at risk management. In relation to options this comes down to understanding the Greeks and the typical model risk involved.

Q: Are you trying to say this is a book about models and complicated formulas?
A: No, not at all. I take the Black–Scholes model, which is the most basic option model used in the industry, and explain the model from a very intuitive point of view.

Q: So there are no formulas or mathematics in your book...
A: Not true; there are formulas but only when they make sense. The level of mathematics is elementary so I can focus on concepts rather than deep mathematical results. I provide plenty of references throughout the book for the reader who wants to find out more afterwards.

Q: What is the target audience?
A: The audience is pretty wide as sometimes there is a gap between theory and practice. A lot of books focus on exotic models or very complicated problems of the industry and at the same time there is sometimes a communication gap between traders who manage the risks of options, risk managers, regulators, quantitative analysts and executive management. This book takes the time to align several worlds by focusing on intuition without sacrificing accuracy or relevance.

Q: How did you decide to write this book?
A: It started off as an internal training I gave in a trading environment. I was working as a derivatives quantitative analyst and we had hired a whole bunch of new people who had various backgrounds and were lacking specific derivatives trading knowledge. This training rolled into a university course, a post-graduate programme and industry workshops over the next years. The book is the final outcome of all this training. A

lot of the concepts and insights I still use on a daily basis when interacting with risk, management, strategy or traders.

Q: So it focuses on building intuition?
A: Yes, that's correct.

Q: But I have been working in the financial industry for several years. Is this still useful for me?
A: I believe so, as some of the topics are presented differently. In some cases I formalise the way traders have been working and thinking for a long time. The combination of structuring and pricing experience, as well as trading derivatives in liquid and illiquid markets, has helped me to bring all this together when discussing basic and advanced topics around options.

Q: How many different models do you treat in this book?
A: The binomial tree model is treated briefly as it explains the cost of hedging concept very well. After that, almost all focus goes to the Black–Scholes model. But I show that the model is not perfect.

Q: You show that a model is not perfect? Why do you do this?
A: Because when you understand what the limitations of a model are, you can use it as a powerful tool. In fact, the industry has adapted to these shortcomings and traders know and understand how the model should be modified. We present several examples of how to adjust in such a way that they make sense and help the reader connect the dots. We touch on some more exotic models, but I chose to deepen the intuition in one model rather than switching to more advanced mathematics.

Q: I still didn't understand the hedging part of your title?
A: I elaborate on the fact that the price of an option or derivative is directly linked to the cost of hedging. This might seem counterintuitive and there are some examples in this book that explain this better. Once this is understood, it makes sense to dedicate a lot of time to the hedging techniques of options. This inevitably leads to the concept of the Greeks.

Q: So the Greeks are the hedging numbers? I always heard they are the partial derivatives of the option price with respect to the price, interest rate, and so on.
A: They are, but that's not the intuitive way of looking at them. The first thing I learned myself when working as a quantitative analyst amongst traders is that this is not how traders look at the Greeks. They see them as exposures and understand how they will dynamically change over time or when the market moves.

Q: So you will teach us to understand traders' lingo?
A: Yes.

Q: Will we learn about volatility?
A: Yes, I will have a lot to say about volatility. There are even exercises that make you think further and deeper about all the important concepts.

Q: Does the book focus on a particular asset class?
A: The whole book is formulated in terms of equity derivatives, but all the concepts are applicable in other markets such as Foreign Exchange (FX), interest rates and commodities. In fact the initial training that is the foundation of the book was around energy derivatives. It just made more sense to focus on one asset class and to develop the intuition around hedging, the Greeks, the volatility and the replication cost rather than explaining particular conventions in a particular market. There are other books in the Finance Explained series that cope with the details of those markets.

Q: That sounds all very exciting... I can't wait to start...
A: Don't let me stall you. The book is all yours now.

Short overview

This book provides an intuitive perspective on the hedging of options. It is common to decompose the exposures of an option into the so-called Greeks. These Greeks measure the sensitivities of the option value with respect to all market parameters. If the behaviour and interplay of the Greeks is well understood, derivatives have no more secrets. In Chapter 1, it will be shown that the hedging cost fully determines the price of an option. As a first step, the focus will be on model-independent results such as the forward price of a stock or the Put-Call parity. Furthermore, the binomial tree model will be introduced. Although not very useful in practice, it comprises the essentials one has to understand before moving on to a more useful model. In particular, it is easy to demonstrate that direction or drift of a stock has no influence on the price of an option. This is an essential property that forms the foundation of the derivatives industry. Chapter 1 will also introduce the celebrated Black–Scholes model, sometimes also referred to as the Black–Scholes–Merton model. The chapter is finalised by the introduction of some elementary concepts and notation.

When diving into Chapter 2, the reader will encounter the *delta* hedging method. In a theoretical setting this is a technique that allows for dynamic replication of the risk of a derivatives payout such as an option. Of course, when dealing with a model one should always understand its assumptions and more importantly its limitations. For example, practical considerations such as discrete hedging, slippage, noise around parameter estimation all lead to a hedging error. All this is very closely entangled with the volatility of the underlying asset.

In Chapter 3 the decomposition of the option price in two other Greeks will be outlined. The *gamma* measures the hedging error introduced by the delta ratio and the *theta* expresses the value loss over time. It will be shown that the combined knowledge of these three Greeks captures enough information to price any option or portfolio of options. This is all linked back to the hedging problem. It is therefore crucial to appreciate the shape and form these three Greeks can take, and the rest of the chapter is devoted to developing an intuition around its profile and behaviour, which concludes the basic theory of the book.

After first challenging and undermining all the assumptions of the Black–Scholes model in Chapter 4 with a series of examples and analysis, the question of why this model is still useful is addressed. This interesting paradox reinforces the Black–Scholes approach and, from both an educational and practical perspective, there is value to be found in this model, which is the reason why the market adopted it as the standard, although not blindly. In fact, the flaws and shortcomings are embraced because they are well understood and, by simple extensions and tricks, the model remains an adequate instrument.

Chapter 5 is devoted to the most important Greek of all, the *vega*. This Greek is related to the volatility and, as will be shown, the vega is connected to the Black–Scholes model rather than to a market parameter. Over time, the market has developed and the volatility parameter became a market parameter rather than just a number in a model. Because of this, the chapter will spend a considerable amount of time studying the Greeks that were introduced earlier under changing volatility values.

After all the Greeks have been introduced and their dynamics properties are analysed, the decomposition of the option price in terms of all the Greeks is investigated. Chapter 6 uses the Taylor expansion to do this. Rather than turning this into a theoretical chapter, the expansion is used to explain the P&L of a derivatives book. Once the dynamics of the options is recognised, the step towards delta-gamma-theta-vega hedging is very quickly taken.

The last two chapters treat more advanced topics. In Chapter 7 the term structure of volatility is revealed. Options with different expiration dates will experience a different path of the underlying stock because of the duration of the option. So it is not unexpected that the calculation for determining the cost of hedging results in a different value for the volatility. The real puzzle is how to rhyme this with the hedging procedure.

In Chapter 8 the hedging approach is taken one step further, and it will be shown how to incorporate risk premiums into the option price. A series of examples are presented to explain how to price in additional risks in the hedging procedure. This very naturally leads to smile and skew in the volatility. This implies that options with different strikes are priced and hedged with a variety of volatilities. Of course there are limitations as to how far this can be stretched and the rules of the game are presented across different maturities. The whole set of volatilities across different strikes and maturities contributes to the implied volatility surface.

1
Hedging Contingent Claims

1.1 Introduction

In this chapter we will present a few simple examples that show what hedging is all about. In practice, understanding how to hedge risks is the single most important factor to become a good trader. In the general public traders, and in particular traders who are working with derivatives like options, are considered to be big risk takers [117, 31]. On some occasions, history has demonstrated that options can be tricky financial instruments that can introduce huge losses for the banks or institutions trading them [149, 117, 55]. However, the flexibility that these instruments bring to the investors or professional players in terms of reducing their risk cannot be denied [58, 52]. Therefore, it is critical that both academics and practitioners develop a thorough understanding of both the theory, the market, the applications and the shortcomings or assumptions of the various models that are being deployed.

As we progress through the different chapters, we will develop a deeper understanding of how a trader looks at various aspects of these instruments. There will be different steps of understanding. First of all, the fact that the price of such an instrument has a life of its own should never be neglected. Usually there is a model price that sets a range of prices, but as the instrument gets offered in the market, depending on the appetite of the other participants, the price might be pushed to its boundaries. Two observations need to be made here that are vitally important. First, the model starts from a set of assumptions. Usually, most of these assumptions can be challenged, as we will see throughout this book. We will start from a very strict set of assumptions, and then gradually relax them, leading the reader more and more in the direction of the real market. It can and has happened that a certain model [18] becomes the market standard although the basic assumptions are violated. If the market is well developed, this does not have to be a problem, because most participants know how to adjust their pricings to accommodate for this deficiency. This is the case for plain vanilla call and put options and the Black–Scholes model. We will discuss this in detail through the next chapters. The model can still provide a guideline to help the trader set his price. We will argue later that the real price of a derivative is determined by the cost of hedging and the residual risk. Both depend on the strategy the trader wishes to follow once the instrument becomes part of his book.

The second observation to bear in mind is that there can be situations where the model's assumptions are wrong in the sense that they do not capture all of the essential risks. The situation can become even worse when this particular model becomes the market standard, leading to a misunderstanding of the price of the instrument by some participants [47]. This has been the case in the credit market with the valuation of products such as Collateralised Debt Obligations (CDO) [134]. It is important not to get a false sense of comfort because a model is available. When the boundaries of a model are well understood, it usually is a very useful tool [144].

This means that at all times the model should be questioned. However, how to model derivatives in more advanced ways will be beyond the scope of this book, as there are many books available that discuss in high mathematical detail how to set up different models [96, 22, 17, 36], depending on the particular asset class, instrument or market feature one is trying to capture [133, 122, 44, 124].

The focus of this book is to explain, once the risk has been taken by the trader and a transaction in this instrument is done, how to manage this risk properly. This brings us to the next step of understanding. We will start by setting up laboratory conditions such that it becomes possible to reduce the risk to almost zero. This is how a derivatives trader looks at his book, containing all different risks, at least as a first step. In principle his starting point is to manage and reduce, and if possible eliminate, the risks. For this, he will set up a trading strategy and typically the cost of this strategy should correspond to the price of the financial instrument.

Furthermore, the trader will take more active positions and challenge the current market levels of both the underlying asset and the model parameters. At this point, the trader starts taking on a risk. In later chapters we will show how the market adjusts every day, based on new information that becomes available. This flow of information leads to more insight and can lead to the understanding that the initial assessment of the price for the model parameters were not entirely correct and should be adjusted.

In this book, we will always look at the viewpoint of the trader who is willing to buy or sell any financial instrument to provide service to a client. The motivations for the client are endless and can go from reducing his risk through securing margins to speculation. Let us give an example of each one of these situations.

A pension fund may have built up huge positions in the stock market and wish to protect themselves from a short-term drop in the equity market. Rather than unwinding their entire portfolio, which would also mean giving up the upside potential, the fund manager can decide to buy an insurance against a sudden drop. For that, he will pay a premium that would pay back any drop below 10 per cent of the stock market. The financial instrument that the fund manager would buy from the trader is a put option, as we will define later.

A second example is a company that is located in Europe but exporting to the US. After signing the contract for delivery of the goods at a certain price, the company knows that he will receive a future cashflow in dollars, whereas his costs are in euros. In the negotiation, the current level of the FX rate has been taken into account, but if the dollar weakens the transaction might lose its profitability. Therefore, the company might wish to fix the current level of the FX rate and turn to a trader to step into a forward FX contract, ensuring him that at the future date when the client pays for his goods, he can exchange the dollar transaction into euros at the current levels.

A third example would be a speculant that enters into the market purely on a direction view. He might think that the stock market is currently at a historical low level and, rather than investing directly into the stocks, he chooses to invest into call options on the stocks. Typically the premium to such an option is relatively low compared to the stock price and the leveraged returns that are possible are enormous. However, there is a risk that the premium gets lost and the investor loses all of his investment.

However, the trader is in yet another position, as he offers this flexibility to any of the above participants, but he cannot afford to bet on the market like the speculant is doing, nor does he have the underlying portfolio to cover for the insurance in case the pension fund managers call upon his claim. This brings us nicely to the need for hedging. The trader will take over the risk and use his insights and large scale to hedge the risks, securing his own viability.

1.2   Setting Some Notation

Throughout the book, we will always refer to the price of a stock or index as S and, when relevant, we will explicitly mention the time dependence (or observation time) by using $S(t)$. Typically we will omit the time dependence if we are focusing on the situations where the time is fixed as a moving component. The current time will be denoted as t_0 and hence the current price level is denoted as $S(t_0)$. Very often we will want to use the short-cut notation $S_0 = S(t_0)$ if we want to focus more on the initial level than on the time aspect. In many applications there will be future expiries or time horizons. We will denote these by a capital T.

The notation t and T are used to refer to specific times. Very often we will need the duration which we will denote as $\tau = \tau(t, T) = T - t$ and it refers to the duration from t to T. In most of the theoretical considerations we will just use the short notation τ but in practical applications we will elaborate a bit on the different ways one can calculate this duration.

For almost all applications, we will assume we can accumulate interests at a constant rate r in a continuously compounding setting. This means that we get interests on interests immediately. The reason is that this makes the notation more slick and our focus will be on the hedging of options, not so much on the interest rate conventions that are used throughout the industry.

If the stock pays out a dividend, we will use q as the notation for the continuously compounded dividend yield. Both the interest rate r and the dividend yield will occur in the exponential function $\exp(\cdot)$ because of the continously compounding assumption. The inverse mathematical function is the natural logarithm and this will be denoted by $\log(\cdot)$.

Later on we will define financial derivative instruments such as options [89]. Their price will always be denoted by π, where we will use a subscript notation if we want to indicate explicitly which the instrument is, that is we will use π_C for the price of a call option and π_P for the price of a put option. As with the stock price, we will often add the explicit time dimension $\pi(t)$. However, since these instruments are derivatives, they are also dependent on the stock price level. We should therefore write $\pi(S, t)$ where of course we mean $\pi(S(t), t)$ but for ease of notation we will often omit the time dependency in the stock, particularly if we are trying to focus on the dependency of the derivatives price for a particular price level of the stock.

Derivatives have a strike price K (which will be defined in Section 1.4) and sometimes we will explicitly incorporate this, as well as the expiry date T, into the notation $\pi(S(t), t; K, T)$. When discussing option prices with different strikes and maturities, we will on occasion omit the dependence on current time and stock level when it will be clear from the context.

Although we will sometimes flip from one notation to another, the context should always be clear. When using a larger portfolio and not just looking at one particular instrument, we will use V for its value or price process. And of course we will very often explicitly denote $V = V(S,t)$ or $V(S(t),t)$. Furthermore, when the value of the portfolio or derivative instrument depends on other (model) parameters, which in our case will typically be the volatility σ (see Chapter 2), we will include this in the notation and write $V(S,t,\sigma)$ or $\pi(S,t,\sigma)$. Once again we might explicitly mention the dependence of the stock price on time if this is relevant within the context.

The cumulative normal distribution function will be denoted by $N(\cdot)$ and the corresponding standard normal density function as $\phi(\cdot)$.

1.3 Hedging Forwards

One of the most simple instruments to hedge is a forward contract [89]. A forward is an agreement between two parties to buy or sell an asset at a certain time in the future, at a fixed agreed price. The future time is called the expiry or expiration date and we will denote this as T. Usually the fixed price is set such that there is no cost to the contract when signing, postponing all cashflows to the future. Let us turn to an example to clarify this way of working. Suppose the underlying asset is a listed stock, for which we denote the price at any given time t as $S(t)$. As this is a listed stock, this price information is available to all parties. Suppose however a client wishes to postpone the payment because he only needs to have the stock in the future, but has observed that the current levels are quite low and wishes to profit from this.

The client and the trader want to agree on the price in the future, which for now we will denote as K. If the trader knows that the client wants to have the stock delivered to him in the future, say at time T, the strategy for him to follow is to buy the stock immediately in the market. This will lock in the current market level and hence eliminate the market risk.

However, this requires the trader to do a transaction and will lead to a cashflow. Either the trader has the money to do this, but in this case he cannot use this money for other purposes anymore, so there is an opportunity loss, or the trader does not have the money, and needs to borrow in order to do his transaction. Both situations lead to the same result if there is only one fixed interest rate available. We will assume that the interest rate is fixed at r, regardless of the direction (loan or savings account) or the tenor (lifetime). The amount the trader needs to borrow is the price of the stock $S(t_0)$ if t_0 is today. The trader will pay back his loan at the time when the client will buy the stock from the trader, which was denoted by T. So at that time, there will be two cashflows. First, the client will pay K to the trader and the trader has to pay back his loan, which would be his capital requirement and the accrued interest, resulting in the amount of $S(t_0) \cdot \exp(r(T - t_0))$. So in order to balance out any risks, the trader has to make sure that the payment he will get from his client is enough to pay back his loan. This means that K should be equal to:

$$K = S(t_0) \cdot \exp(r(T - t_0)). \tag{1.1}$$

A lower value for K would mean that the trader could not pay back his loan and would see a loss in this transaction, which would obviously prevent him from doing this in the first place. A higher value of K would lead to a sure profit for the trader, but will most likely push away the client to another party who will give him a better deal. Clearly, in real life, there are always small margins that come hand in hand with the service provided to the client.

Very interesting to notice is that the trader does not take any stand in what he thinks the direction of the market is. And regardless of what the value of the stock is at time T, his risks are neutralised. In other words, he is fully hedged. Like predicted earlier, the cost of the hedging construction leads to the forward value K. This leads us to the conclusion that a trader who is servicing the clients for fixing forward prices does not even have to have a directional view over the market. He does not take any risks if he sticks to this strategy to neutralise the risk. However, a more experienced trader might take timing and volume into account. He might price the forward according to (1.1), but at the same time postpone his hedge if he expects the stock price to drop even lower during the next hours or days. At that point, he is taking a risk. If he turns out to be right, he can buy the stock at a lower price than the one he used for pricing the contract for his client, leading to a smaller loan and a profit on the deal. However, if he turns out to be wrong he will have to buy the stock at a higher price, which obviously will result in a loss.

Once we turn to real stocks, the problem becomes more complicated [152] as it is typical for some stocks to pay dividends [113] to the holder of the stock. Suppose that the dividend is paid out by the company to the holder at time t_1 and we assume that this happens before the exchange of the stock between the trader and the client. Clearly, as the client will only get the stock delivered to him after this dividend has been paid out he cannot claim the dividend. However, in his hedging strategy, the trader has purchased the stock, so he will receive an extra cashflow in the amount of the dividend. After he receives this payment, he can leave that money in his account where it will accrue interests. It becomes clear that in this case, his cost of hedging will reduce. Suppose the dividend payment is denoted by D. The fair value of the forward price he should charge his client would then be

$$K = S(t_0) \cdot \exp\left(r\left(T - t_0\right)\right) - D\exp\left(r\left(T - t_1\right)\right). \tag{1.2}$$

This however leads us to an interesting setup, as the value of the dividend payment is often not known in advance. Most often the company announces the value of the dividend, if any, a few months before the payment. However, forward contracts can be signed with delivery several years from now, and it then becomes an extra risk for the trader to estimate the value of the dividends during the hedging period.

When this becomes relevant we leave the laboratory setup, and the risks for the trader cannot be hedged perfectly. What will happen is that he will estimate the dividend payments as well as he can and probably try to underestimate them, so that he won't be facing unpleasant surprises down the hedging road. Very interestingly, what will happen exactly is that the client will search for the trader who will give him the best deal and, in liquid, transparent markets, this will lead to a market consensus on the future dividend value. This goes as follows. Suppose trader A is very conservative and estimates the value of the dividend D very low, almost zero, whereas trader B estimates the dividend to be quite high.

What will happen is that one client after the other will contact both trader A and B and always do the transaction with trader B. Trader A will receive no business, probably making him wonder if his estimate is not too conservative. At the same time, trader B will wonder why he closes every single deal. In order to capture some business, trader A will increase his estimate of the dividend, and at the same time trader B will try to make more profit on this type of deal, lowering his estimate for the dividend. This process will continue until trader A will get part of the business flow and trader B will lose out on some deals. That is where the market consensus is then settled.

It is very important to realise that this does not mean that this market consensus on the estimated value D is correct; it is only the consensus. People often say 'the market is always right' but this merely reflects a consensus of the market. Market prices basically represent a balance where different participants meet each other in an equilibrium. Of course this equilibrium is usually very short-lived and prices therefore change constantly.

External factors to make the market participants (and hence the market) change their point of view can be of various natures. First of all, the available information on a particular stock can change, and as a consequence the stock value or the estimate on the dividend can change. In times where company profits are increasing year by year, most traders are optimistic that the future dividends will be higher than the past ones. However, a change in the economic situation can turn the sentiment very rapidly. Second, the interest in this particular product will trigger the traders as well. If there is only one request for such a product, and the deal is lost, there will be no incentive for adjusting the current estimates. However, if there is a lot of business flow that the trader is missing out on, he might be more tempted to revise his assumptions. Third, the risk appetite of the trader plays an important role. How much risk is he willing to take. What might be undesirable is to pile up identical risks in your books, because if you are wrong it will lead to a catastrophe in your book. So typically, a trader might be more aggressive when this is the first deal he would get of this kind, but as the deals pile up he will become more conservative. He will demand more value for the same risk, as it adds on to the risks that are already present in his book.

If there is more than one dividend payment before the time horizon is reached, we have to bring in more assumptions on each of the dividend payments D_i with dividend payment dates t_i and $i = 1, \ldots, N$. The fair-value price then becomes

$$K = S(t_0) \exp\left(r(T - t_0)\right) - \sum_{i=1}^{N} D_i \exp\left(r(T - t_i)\right).$$

In the limit, where the stream of dividends is continuous rather than discrete, it makes sense to describe the dividend payments as a percentage of the current stock level. In this framework of a continuous dividend yield q, the forward price for a stock reformulates to

$$K = S(t_0) \cdot \exp\left((r - q)(T - t_0)\right). \tag{1.3}$$

1.4 What Are Calls and Puts?

Before we continue, we formally introduce what a call and put option really is. These so-called derivative instruments [89] have a payout function that is completely determined by another underlying financial asset, such as a stock price or index level.

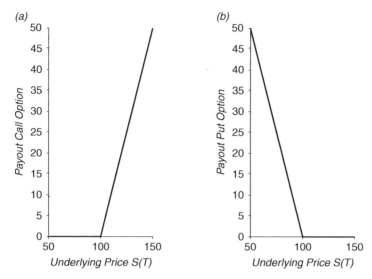

Figure 1.1 The payout profile with strike $K = 100$ as a function of the terminal stock price $S(T)$ for (a) a call option and (b) a put option.

Call options give the holder the right to buy the underlying instrument for a fixed price at a given instant in the future. Put options give the holder the right to sell the underlying at a fixed price at a given instant in the future. The fixed price is referred to as the strike price or exercise price and will be denoted by K. The future time where the right ends and the holder needs to decide whether or not he exercises is called the expiry or the maturity, and we will denote this as T.

The payout formula that gives the value of an option contract is a very easy, non-linear function given by

$$(S(T) - K)^+ = \max(S(T) - K, 0) \tag{1.4}$$

for a call option and

$$(K - S(T))^+ = \max(K - S(T), 0) \tag{1.5}$$

for a put option. Both profiles can be seen in Figure 1.1 and, because of the specific shape, people often refer to these profiles as the hockey-stick profiles.

If we focus on the put option as an example, we see that the holder has the right to sell the underlying instrument at a predetermined price as stated above. When will the holder use his right to exercise? If the price $S(T)$ at the moment of exercise is above the strike price K, the holder of the option will not use the option, so the option is said to expire worthless. In the other case, when $S(T)$ is below the strike K, the holder will use his right.

In the market, there are cash-settled and physically-settled options. Cash-settled options will induce a cashflow of the value calculated from (1.4) or (1.5). In case an option is physically settled, there will be an exchange of the physical stock (of course by electronic means) and a cashflow of the amount K.

In the market there are a couple of common options available [89, 52]. The option defined above is known as a plain vanilla European option. The European refers to the fact that the only moment of exercise is at the expiry date of the option, not to the geographical location it is traded in. European options are traded all over the globe, on a wide variety of underlying instruments such as currency pairs, stock indices, single stocks, interest rates, bonds, commodities ...

There is a class of options where the exercise is not restricted to the expiry but in fact the options can be exercised on any (trading) day. These are known as American options [49]. Unlike European options, this class of product does not have a closed-form formula available, making them slightly harder to manage. We will focus on the European equivalent. There are many more exotic variants available in the market. For example, Bermudan options are options that can be exercised more often than just at the expiry date, but not as often as American options.

More exotic structures such as barriers are traded as well. These are call and put options that can be knocked in or out of existence depending on a criterion that gets monitored continuously or at predescribed times. Lookback options are options where the strike price is not set in advance but is in fact again a formula that depends on the price behaviour of the stock during the entire lifetime or certain observation windows. The risk profiles for these exotic options are typically more complicated than for plain vanilla European options but the analysis requires a solid understanding of the basic building blocks, which are those simple derivatives.

1.5 Pricing and Hedging Options in the Binomial Tree model

We treated the simple case of hedging forwards and we will now move to a more complicated instrument, but again start from a controlled lab experiment. As stated in Section 1.4 a call option is a financial instrument that allows the holder to buy the underlying asset at a fixed future time T, for a fixed price K. A very important difference between an option and a forward is the fact that the holder has the choice to either take the asset at the price K or waive the contract. This brings an asymmetry into the picture, as he will choose to optimise.

Suppose the holder of the option really wants to obtain the stock at time T. In case the value of the stock at that time is lower than K, which is the price at which he can buy from the trader, he will simply ignore his right to do so, go into the stock market, and pay $S(T)$ for the stock. However, if at that time the stock price is higher than K he will of course claim from the trader to receive the stock at price K.

From the traders point of view, it is clear that hedging cannot be done as simply as before, as he doesn't know in advance whether or not the client will claim his stock. In the context of the Black–Scholes model [18], we will explain how this hedging strategy needs to be adjusted dynamically in order to accommodate for the changing risk profile. For now, we will just focus on a very simple example [40] where the future price uncertainty is limited to two possible outcomes. This means that the hedge should stand the test of these outcomes only. Note that this is a strong assumption, which is unrealistic in practice, but we will discuss it anyway as it will provide us with more insight on what hedging is. Later on, when we use a more useful model, the same principles will still hold.

Before we introduce the mathematics of the model, let us focus on an example (see Figure 1.2). Suppose we are looking at a stock with current value $S_0 = S(t_0) = 100$ and

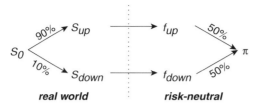

Figure 1.2 A schematic representation of the binomial tree model. The stock price has two possible outcomes in a predetermined timestep. For each of these, we can calculate unambiguously the value of the derivative. These values can then be combined into the risk-neutral price of the derivative.

suppose at the maturity of the call option there are only two possible outcomes, namely a high value of $S(T) = S_{up} = 110$ and a low value of $S(T) = S_{down} = 90$. Suppose we also know the probability for each of those outcomes in the sense that the probability the stock moves to its the high value is $q = 90\%$ and the probability it moves down is only $1 - q = 10\%$.

For the strike of the call option, we assume a value of $K = 100$. This means that in the high value scenario, the holder of the call option can purchase the stock from the trader for 100, and immediately resell it into the market for 110, as this is the market level at that time. It is clear that the value of this derivative is 10, the difference between the market level and the strike price. However, in case the less likely event occurs that the stock decreases to 90, the client would not exercise his option. The option is worthless and the right to exercise will be waived.

So, we can summarise that there are two possible outcomes, for which we can assess both the value of the stock (model assumption) and the value of the call option. Looking at this from a statistical point of view, we can say that the holder of the call option has a 90% chance of gaining 10 by holding the contract, and a 10% chance of zero value. The mean or average value is clearly 9. So, if this were just a game of chance, this would be a fair value premium for the contract. However, quite surprisingly, we will now show that the trader can sell this option to the client much cheaper because of hedging principles. In particular, it will become obvious that his cost of hedging will be just 5, being the equally weighted average of the payout over all different scenarios, disregarding the real probabilities.

In the market, options are often not sold individually, but in larger units of 2, 10 or 100. Of course, traded volumes are often much larger and notional amounts changing hands are millions. For simplicity, we will disregard this fact now but as a consequence assume that you can trade fractions of stocks, such as half a stock and so on. The reader who finds this assumption disturbing just has to think that one unit corresponds to larger volumes. Below, we will retake this example in formulas and derive exactly how this hedging strategy is determined, but for now we will keep the magic and just reveal that the trader, once having sold this contract for 5, will buy in the market 0.5 stocks at the current market level. To simplify even further in this example, we will assume the trader can borrow money for free and does not gain any interest on money he has. Shortly, we will relax these restrictions. So the portfolio or book of the trader consists of three parts: his bank account, a position in the stock and a position in the option.

At present or t_0, the cashflows are as follows: the trader receives 5 for selling the option, takes a loan of 45 to pay for the stock and buys half of the stock, paying 50.

Now, let us analyse both possible scenarios separately, starting with the most likely one. The stock has gone up to 110, and we know that the client will call the trader to claim his stock. Since the trader only owns half of a stock, he will have to buy the other half. This results in another negative cashflow of 55, bringing his loan to a total amount of 100. However the client pays the strike price of 100, which exactly settles the loan of the trader. Clearly, he was fully hedged against this scenario and he didn't suffer any costs (or gains). The trader was not at risk in this scenario.

Now, let us turn to the other scenario where the stock price decreases. In this case, the client will not claim the stock and the communication with this client will finish. The trader will clear his position by selling half the stock he had bought as a precaution. However since this value went down, he will only get back 45 from this transaction. However, this just covers the loan he still has. So again, it turns out that the trader was fully hedged against this outcome as well.

Any value above 5 would have led to a surplus or a profit on the trader's behalf. It is a nice example of how the cost of the hedging construction sets the price, whereas the client might be willing to pay much more for this contract as he also takes into account the probabilities of the future outcomes. Sometimes, it is assumed that knowing the value of call and put options of several strikes leads to information on the expectance of the market on future values of the stock. This example shows that one has to be careful in this assumption. We will come back to this in Chapter 8.

We have now looked at the example from the more physical point of view, meaning that we explained how the trader had to buy another half of the stock before being able to turn it over to the client. However, for all future purposes it is much more convenient to look at it from a financial point of view. This means that we say the trader has to pay out the value of the call option to the client, rather than handing over the stock to him. This means that he can clear his position in the stock first, cash in the 55 that it is worth, pay out the client his 10 and pay back the loan of 45 with the remainder. Obviously, the result is the same, but it is just a different perspective.

Before we turn to the more general case, let us recap the major assumptions that led us to disregard the actual probabilities of the future states. The vital assumptions were that the fluctuations from the current level were known, there was no interest to be paid on the loan and finally, that you could freely buy or sell the stock underlying to the call option contract. Although the model is extremely simple and only useful for clarifying the hedging concept, these assumptions will turn out to be the essential ones that allow a trader to manage his risks, even in real life situations.

The next part of this section, will formalise the above example to reveal the magic of how we got to the correct hedge. It is already clear that this 50 per cent value was apparently the correct one, as it is the only one that covers the future cashflows in both situations without exposing the trader to any risk. We will take some distance from the example of the call option and assume that the trader sold a particular derived instrument that gives a payout of f_{up} in case the stock went up to S_{up} and a payout of f_{down} in the down scenario where the stock is worth S_{down}. The instrument can be a call or put, with any strike or even a forward.

So at time t_0, when the trader sells the derivative, he has to buy a certain amount of stocks, let us say Δ stocks. The value of this Δ is the real magic of the game. In order to find this, we will just demand that the trader is hedged against both possible outcomes. We know in advance that the trader will receive the premium π from selling the derivative, which can be deducted from the loan he has to take to buy the Δ stocks (at a value of S_0). So the initial loan is $\Delta \cdot S_0 - \pi$, to be paid back at time T. Suppose the interest rate is r; then the actual amount that needs to be paid back is given by $\exp(r(T - t_0))(\Delta \cdot S_0 - \pi)$. This amount is the same, regardless of the outcome of the world. What makes the difference is the value of the stock, and the value of the derivative. In the up scenario, the trader's book is worth $\Delta \cdot S_{up} - f_{up}$ (excluding the loan) and in the down scenario we obtain a similar expression $\Delta \cdot S_{down} - f_{down}$.

Hedging is all about neutralising the effect of the different outcomes. So what the trader wants is a book value in the future that is independent of the value of the stock, as this is the uncertainty parameter in the picture. We can do this by setting the value Δ such that we do indeed obtain identical book values in both scenarios:

$$\Delta \cdot S_{up} - f_{up} = \Delta \cdot S_{down} - f_{down}$$

$$\Rightarrow \Delta = \frac{f_{up} - f_{down}}{S_{up} - S_{down}},$$

which clearly is independent of the probabilities of the up and down move.

Once we have obtained the number of stocks we need to purchase as a hedge in the initial step, it is easy to figure out the exact premium that we need to charge for that. As we know how much the trader's book will be worth at time T (remember it does not depend on the outcome of the world because of the hedging procedure), we can take this value into account, together with the loan he has to pay back, and demand that this is a zero-cost operation. Hence

$$\exp(r(T - t_0))(\Delta \cdot S(t_0) - \pi) = \Delta \cdot S_{up} - f_{up}.$$

We could have used the expression with the down move of the stock on the right-hand side of the equation as it is identical in value. Backing out the one value of the premium that leads to a zero cost and filling in the value of Δ that we derived earlier, together with using the duration $\tau = T - t_0$, brings us to:

$$\pi = \Delta \cdot S_0 - \exp(-r\tau)(\Delta \cdot S_{up} - f_{up})$$

$$= \frac{(f_{up} - f_{down})S_0 - \exp(-r\tau)((f_{up} - f_{down})S_{up} - f_{up}(S_{up} - S_{down}))}{S_{up} - S_{down}}$$

$$= \frac{(f_{up} - f_{down})S_0 - \exp(-r\tau)(f_{up}S_{down} - f_{down}S_{up})}{S_{up} - S_{down}}.$$

Most often within this model, called the binomial tree model [40], the up and down moves are written as a function of the original value of the stock: $S_{up} = S_0 \cdot u$ and $S_{down} = S_0 \cdot d$. This simplifies the formula substantially:

$$\pi = \frac{(f_{up} - f_{down}) - \exp(-r\tau)(f_{up}d - f_{down}u)}{u - d}$$

$$= \exp(-r\tau)\left(\frac{\exp(r\tau) - d}{u - d}f_{up} + \frac{-\exp(r\tau) + u}{u - d}f_{down}\right).$$

For convenience write

$$p = \frac{\exp(-r\tau) - d}{u - d}$$

and we then obtain easily that

$$1 - p = 1 - \frac{\exp(-r\tau) - d}{u - d}$$
$$= \frac{u - \exp(-r\tau)}{u - d}.$$

From all this, we obtain the value of the premium in the following intuitive formula (where we switched from the duration notation τ back to the explicit reference of times t_0 and expiry T):

$$\pi = \exp(-r(T - t_0)) \left(p \cdot f_{up} + (1 - p) \cdot f_{down}\right). \tag{1.6}$$

Let's analyse this formula, or at least the format of it. At first sight, it looks like a discounted average over the expected payouts of the claim (the derivative). But we started this section by saying this was a false argument and that the actual price was set by the cost of hedging rather than by calculating the expectation value. This statement is still true, as the artificial value of p is coming from the construction and is a result of the model, rather than the statistical nature of the problem. Because of the way it looks, it is called the discounted risk-neutral expectation value, where clearly the risk-neutral part of this expression is coming from the fact that the trader does not have any risk at all.

Another amazing observation is the fact that within this expression of p, there is no dependence on the actual derivative that you are pricing. This means that this formula is valid for any derivative on the same stock. Mathematicians call this p still a probability measure under which all your pricing becomes simple and directly linked to a hedging argument.

At the start of this section, we stated that this model is obviously too simple for all practical purposes. The main failure of the model is the fact that there are only two possible outcomes within the model. This however can be improved by adding many time steps between t_0 and T, all of which allow an up or a down move. Each time step is assumed to have a duration Δt. If we assume an up move followed by a down move (and vice versa) resulting in the original value, or $u = 1/d$, the tree that is built that way is called recombining [131]. Within this extended model it is still possible to start at the final step T and calculate back the premium at the previous step as we did above. Once we have obtained the premium in all possible nodes of this last-but-one step, we can repeat the argument and calculate our way recursively through the tree to end up at time t_0. Clearly the hedging procedure remains intact, but will change from node to node, leading to a dynamic strategy.

In practice, when trying to construct a binomial tree model we will need to find the parameters u and d to match market reality as well as possible. This means we will want to match the expected return μ and the volatility σ of the stock. These parameters are calibrated such that for each timestep Δt, the expected stock price $S_0 (1 + \mu \Delta t)$ and the variance of the price process $(\sigma S_0)^2 \Delta t$ match the expressions in the binomial model. In the next chapter we will come back very extensively to the volatility parameter σ but for now we hope the reader can accept the definition that it is related to the variance of the price process.

Within the binomial tree model, we denote the probability of an upwards move by q and the probability of a downward move by $1 - q$. In the above example we used

$q = 90\%$ and, as we argued above, this probability did not play an explicit role in the valuation of the derivative and in fact we ended up with expressions that depended on p, which we called the risk-neutral probability.

We now try to find the link between the market parameters μ and σ and the model parameters q, u and d:

$$\begin{cases} S_0 \left(1 + \mu \Delta t\right) = q S_0 u + \left(1 - q\right) S_0 d \\ \sigma^2 S_0^2 \Delta t = q \left(S_0 u\right)^2 + \left(1 - q\right) \left(S_0 d\right)^2 - \left(q S_0 u + \left(1 - q\right) S_0 d\right)^2. \end{cases}$$

Starting from the first relationship, we can consequently find

$$q = \frac{\left(1 + \mu \Delta t\right) - d}{u - d} \tag{1.7}$$

or that the drift and the probabilities in the distribution are linked. So when we concluded earlier that the probabilities had no impact, this is equivalent to saying that the drift or direction of the stock has no impact. This is a very counterintuitive result but it is essential to a lot of models in mathematical finance.

In order for the volatilities to match, we need to have

$$\sigma^2 \Delta t = q u^2 + \left(1 - q\right) d^2 - \left(q u + \left(1 - q\right) d\right)^2$$

or equivalently

$$\sigma^2 \Delta t = q \left(1 - q\right) \left(u - d\right)^2.$$

By substituting (1.7) in this expression, it reduces to

$$\sigma^2 \Delta t = \left(\left(1 + \mu \Delta t\right) - d\right) \left(u - \left(1 + \mu \Delta t\right)\right).$$

This equation has more than one solution, but an obvious one in the recombining tree model is to take

$$\begin{cases} u = 1 + \sigma \sqrt{\Delta t} \\ d = 1 - \sigma \sqrt{\Delta t}. \end{cases}$$

Another solution is

$$\begin{cases} u = \exp\left(\sigma \Delta t\right) \\ d = \exp\left(-\sigma \Delta t\right) \end{cases}$$

which is the framework originally proposed by Cox, Ross and Rubinstein [40]. In neither expression is there a trace of the drift μ nor of the actual probability q.

The multi-step binomial tree model is handled in a lot more detail in any textbook on mathematical finance [136, 96] so we won't spend more time on it here. The Black–Scholes model, which we will introduce next, can be shown [100] to be a limit of the binomial tree model where there is an infinite number of time steps between today t_0 and the expiry T. Therefore, it will be no surprise that there will exist a hedging argument that allows us to calculate the price of a European call and put option.

1.6 Pricing and Hedging Options in the Black–Scholes Model

In this section, we will briefly discuss the results originally obtained by Black and Scholes [18]. Although these results can be found in most textbooks on mathematical finance or derivatives pricing [13, 17, 135, 123] in a lot more detail and rigour, we wish to add them once again as the argument is key to the management of a book of options from a trader's point of view. Without the possibility of hedging this kind of claim, the derivatives industry wouldn't be the same. It is often said that without the results of Black and Scholes it would be impossible to set up hedging strategies, but this is not entirely true, as even in the period before [76] those particular results were published the trading of options was going on. What is more remarkable is that the traders were actually hedging and managing these positions not so differently to what is going on nowadays. This knowledge was considered more an art than a science and was passed on from the expert to the junior, as many crafts were passed on.

While the previous model could be understood with basic knowledge of linear algebra, the Black–Scholes model contains more mathematical complexity. The foundations of the Black–Scholes model are found in a non-trivial extension of classical calculus [61, 120, 147]. We will not focus that much on the mathematical rigour underpinning the theory, but instead just highlight the results we will use later on in the book.

1.6.1   Elimination of the Risk Factor

The starting point for the Black–Scholes model, which we will often refer to as the BS model, is to model the stock price $S(t)$ as a particular random process. The actual dynamics are given in the form of a stochastic differential equation (SDE) [61, 120, 147]

$$dS(t) = \mu S(t)\,dt + \sigma S(t)\,dW(t) \tag{1.8}$$

where μ is called the drift, σ the volatility and $W(t)$ is Brownian motion [100, 126], modelling the noise or uncertainty within the stock price.

The Brownian motion is the (only) continuous process with the following properties.

- It starts off in zero or $W(0) = 0$.
- All non-overlapping increments are independent or in particular $W(t+s) - W(t)$ is independent of $W(t)$.
- All increments are stationary so they only depend on the length of the increment.
- All increments $W(t+s) - W(t)$ are normally distributed with mean zero and variance s. We can denote $W(t+s) - W(t) \sim N(0,s)$ where $N(\cdot,\cdot)$ stands for the normal distribution. We assume that readers are familiar with this distribution [129].

From an intuitive point of view, the stock price move over a time interval is made up of a very large number of small up and down moves that superimposed give the final move. All these up and down moves are considered to be independent and to come from the normal distribution. The main assumptions here in the model are the normal distribution, but also the fact that these increments have no memory effect.

As a consequence of the above properties, the Brownian motion has the following property for its variance:

$$Var[W(t+s)] = Var[W(t) + W(t+s) - W(t)]$$
$$= Var[W(t)] + Var[W(t+s) - W(t)].$$

This property will be important in Chapter 7 when dealing with volatility term structure.

One can actually solve the SDE (1.8), and the solution [100] is given by

$$S(t) = S(t_0) \exp\left(\left(\mu + \frac{1}{2}\sigma^2\right)(t - t_0) + \sigma(W(t) - W(t_0))\right). \tag{1.9}$$

Let us denote the value of the claim on this stock as $\pi(S(t), t)$ where we explicitly mention the dependence on time and of course the stock itself. We cannot derive any of the results without knowing how the dynamics of such a function of the stock is calculated and this result was only found in 1951 by Itô. We will just write it down without justification. It can be considered as a chain rule for stochastic processes, which is different from the classical chain rule in calculus. Itô [120] found that

$$d\pi = \frac{\partial \pi}{\partial S} dS + \frac{\partial \pi}{\partial t} dt + \frac{1}{2}\sigma^2 S^2 dt.$$

If the reader takes this for granted, we can continue along our original path to lay out the hedging argument that is so vital to our understanding of how to manage a book of derivatives. Just like before, the trader will sell a certain claim to a client, for which he receives a premium π. To hedge against the possible movements of the stock, now modelled by this more complicated model, he will buy Δ stocks to protect himself. As we have argued in the extension of the simple one step binomial model into multi steps, this delta depends on where we are in time and we will explicitly write this as $\Delta(t)$. The trader's book consists of a loan, a sold derivative and Δ stocks.

Again, it is more convenient to leave out the loan as this is just a cashflow effect of the calculation and, just as in the previous setting, we don't need it to determine the hedging strategy itself. If we write the value of the book as $V(t)$ at each time t, and the value of the claim as $\pi(S(t), t)$, we know that the change in value of the trader's book comes from the change in the two components, or in other words:

$$dV = \Delta \cdot dS - d\pi.$$

Filling in Itô's result and regrouping gives us the following

$$dV = \Delta dS - \left(\frac{\partial \pi}{\partial S} dS + \frac{\partial \pi}{\partial t} dt + \frac{1}{2}\sigma^2 S^2 dt\right)$$
$$= \left(\Delta - \frac{\partial \pi}{\partial S}\right) dS + \left(\frac{\partial \pi}{\partial t} + \frac{1}{2}\sigma^2 S^2\right) dt.$$

From a hedging point of view, we are looking to eliminate all risks, so we do not want the change in the trader's book to depend on the change in the underlying stock, as this is the factor we cannot predict. To solve this, we just need to select the correct number of stocks to hedge, bringing forward the formula

$$\Delta = \frac{\partial \pi}{\partial S}.$$

However, this does not solve the problem completely, as we don't know the value of the derivative yet and consequently we cannot figure out what the quantity $\partial \pi / \partial S$ is. This, we will present in the next section. It is typical to denote the number of stocks to perform the hedge as the Greek symbol delta. The whole hedging procedure is called delta hedging accordingly [18].

1.6.2 Black–Scholes Results

To derive the actual solution of the problem and to come to the expression of the celebrated Black–Scholes equation would take us too far from the scope of the book [153]. In essence, the arguments [18] are no different from the ones we have presented before. Once the risk is eliminated, the value of the premium π has to compensate for recovering the cost of the hedging procedure. We will omit the actual derivation and refer to the literature [96, 152]. Instead we will just state the resulting formulas for the price of a European call and put option. First denote the following short-hand expressions:

$$F = S(t_0) \exp\left((r - q)(T - t_0)\right)$$

$$d_1 = \frac{\log(F/K) + \frac{1}{2}\sigma^2(T - t_0)}{\sigma\sqrt{T - t_0}}$$

$$d_2 = d_1 - \sigma\sqrt{T - t_0} = \frac{\log(F/K) - \frac{1}{2}\sigma^2(T - t_0)}{\sigma\sqrt{T - t_0}}.$$

We can then summarise the formulas for both the premium and the delta in the tables below [18, 113].

Premium π	
π_C	$\exp(-r(T - t_0))(FN(d_1) - KN(d_2))$
π_P	$\exp(-r(T - t_0))(KN(-d_2) - FN(-d_1))$

(1.10)

Delta Δ	
Δ_C	$\exp(-q(T - t_0))N(d_1)$
Δ_P	$-\exp(-q(T - t_0))N(-d_1)$

(1.11)

As before, q represents the dividend yield (as a percentage) and as before r stands for the interest rate and σ is the volatility parameter. We will have much more to say about the volatility number in the remainder of the book. The formulas above are known as the Black–Scholes formulas for European call and put prices [140].

One remarkable observation is that the option price does not depend on the drift term μ from (1.8). This is the equivalent of the result we had in Section 1.5, where the probability of an up move and down move had absolutely no impact on the option prices. In Figure 1.3 we can observe two different stocks over a period of one year. The stocks have the same current level but we can clearly see that they have been chosen because one has had a downward trend over the last year and the other is on an upward trend. In fact, the paths were constructed with the following parameters:

Stock 1	Stock 2
$\mu_1 = +10\%$	$\mu_2 = -10\%$
$\sigma_1 = 30\%$	$\sigma_2 = 30\%$
$q_1 = 0\%$	$q_2 = 0\%.$

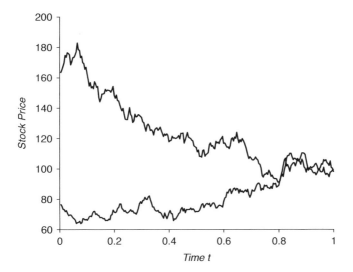

Figure 1.3   The time path of two different stocks. One has a negative trend of -10 per cent and the other has a positive trend of $+10$ per cent. The volatility for both stocks is identical and given by 30 per cent.

The value of a call option with strike $K = 100$ will be just as expensive for both stocks, although historically speaking one stock has a higher probability of ending in the money compared to the other. The reason is that the cost to hedge either option is identical within the Black–Scholes model. We will elaborate much more on this in the subsequent chapters.

In (1.10) and (1.11) we wrote down the BS price formula and the BS delta. In Figure 1.4 we depict in (a) the BS price of a call option versus the intrinsic profile from Figure 1.1. We can see the prices for european call and put options are smooth functions as compared to the digital hockey-stick functions we had for the payout profiles. In the illustration, the call option is against a strike of 105 and the put option has a strike of 95. The interest rate is set at $r = 2\%$ and the dividend yield at $q = 3\%$.

We can also observe the S-shape for the deltas in Figure 1.4(b). At the expiry date, because of the transition point in the strike, the intrinsic delta (or delta at expiry) becomes a digital step function which is zero below the strike and 1 above the strike.

1.6.3   Underlying Distribution

By looking at the option prices in (1.10), we can see that they have the same shape as we derived in the binomial tree model (1.6). We clearly see the discount factor up front and, with a little imagination, one can see the payout functions (1.4) and (1.5) pop up in the Black–Scholes formula.

One of the basic observations that can be proven is that within the Black–Scholes model the distribution of the stock price at expiry date is a lognormal distribution, and one can show that in fact the Black–Scholes formula [16, 133] can be calculated from

$$\pi_C\left(S(t_0), t_0\right) = \exp\left(-r\left(T - t_0\right)\right) \int_0^\infty \max\left(0, s - K\right) \cdot f(s)\, ds \qquad (1.12)$$

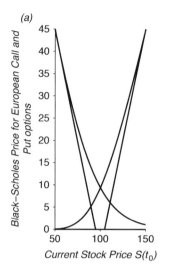 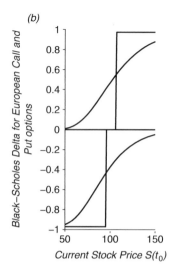

Figure 1.4   (a) The price of a call and put option to be compared to the intrinsic payout profiles. (b) The delta for both the call and put option.

where f is the lognormal density function that describes the distribution of the stock price at the expiry date T. In Chapter 2 we give the exact expression of this density.

After being introduced by Black–Scholes–Merton in the 1970s, this model has been analysed in many different ways by researchers in mathematical finance. This has led to a very deep understanding of the mathematical framework applicable to pricing and hedging options. There are many ways to come to the Black–Scholes formulas and one of them states as above that the option price is the discounted expected value under the risk-neutral probability distribution. This turns out to be true for any option model and forms the basis of much more advanced models that are outside of scope for this book [133].

1.7   Put–Call Parity as a Perfect Hedge

There exists a relationship between the price of a put option and a call option. It is known as the *put–call parity* [102, 71, 99]. This relationship holds in general and is independent of the model used to price options. In fact, any model that does not satisfy this relationship has a clear inconsistency. Let us try and reason our way through the derivation and come up with the relationship in a natural way. The put–call parity gives a link between the price of a put and a call with the same maturity and the same strike. Once we have reached the maturity, the stock has a value either above the strike or below the strike.

So it is economical to exercise either the call option or the put option, but never both at the same time. The most convenient way to proceed is to plot the payout profile or payout function under different scenarios for the stock price at maturity. Suppose the trader bought the call and sold the put. Figure 1.1(*a*) and Figure 1.1(*b*) should then be added on top of each other.

Clearly the two lines in the figures add up to a simple straight line. This would be exactly profit or loss as if the trader had bought the stock at price K, the identical strike price for both the call and put. We can even write this in formula:

$$\pi_C(S(T),T) - \pi_P(S(T),T) = S(T) - K.$$

The reader can easily verify that the actual payout function expresses the same view:

$$\max(S(T) - K, 0) - \max(K - S(T), 0) = S(T) - K.$$

This is (almost) the put–call parity. Now, let's look at this from a hedging point of view. Suppose the trader has bought a call option and sold a put option. How can he hedge this portfolio? We already know what kind of profile he will be exposed to at maturity. In order to replicate this, he just needs to make sure he can sell the stock at K. But wait, that would be too simple, since the stock has its own value and the trader does not get to choose its value.

At maturity he needs to have sold something worth $S(T) - K$. Let us look at the two terms separately. How can he make sure to arrive at the $S(T)$? That is easy, because it is the value of the stock. Although uncertain, the trader knows its current value, which is given by $S(t_0)$. So by selling the stock at t_0, he makes sure he gets that part of the outcome. How does he make sure he has K at time T? He just writes out a loan at t_0 for the amount of $K \cdot \exp(-r(T - t_0))$ which, by the accumulation of interest, will lead to a value of K at maturity.

So if the portfolio with the two options can be replicated statically (hedge is constructed at t_0 and never looked at again, until maturity of the options), then the relationship between the call, put, stock and loan needs to be valid at any time, leading to the following formula:

$$\pi_C(S(t),t) - \pi_P(S(t),t) = S(t) - K\exp(-r(T - t)).$$

This is the general formulation of the put–call parity.

1.8   Some Concepts and Terminology

As part of the derivatives industry, we now need to introduce some vocabulary that is commonly used.

1.8.1   Options can be ITM, OTM or ATM

We introduced the payout formulas (1.4) and (1.5) that were valid at expiry date for the European options. From this we can get the intrinsic value, which can be calculated by evaluating the payout function, but using the current level of the stock, rather than the future (unknown) value. It is the value of the option as if it were to expire right now. We can say that the intrinsic value of a derivative claim is given by

$$\pi(S(t_0), T)$$

and for a call option, for example, this equals $\max(S(t_0) - K, 0)$.

If this intrinsic value is positive, we say that the option is *in-the-money* (ITM) and in the opposite case, we say it is *out-of-the-money* (OTM). Whenever the value of the stock is 'around' the strike level (let's say in a 5 per cent range), we say that the option is *at-the-money* (ATM). Note however that this is just one possible definition for the moneyness. There are other definitions that can be and are used in the industry, depending on the underlying market [89].

Very often people distinguish between the hedging ratio Δ being above or below 50 per cent. The point $\Delta = 50\%$ then is named the ATM point. Note that this does not correspond to the stock and strike being equal. It does however correspond to the delta of the put and the delta of the call being identical. In fact for $S(t) = K$ the delta for a call option is actually typically bigger than 50%. This asymmetry that we see, which was not there in the binomial tree model, has to do with the skew or asymmetry of the lognormal distribution. Because there is a cut-off of the distribution at zero that does not allow the stock to go below zero, there is more probability that the stock will go up, bringing the call option ITM in this second definition. Similarly the put is effectively OTM when $S(t) = K$.

Another point that we would like to mention is the ATM point defined as the forward value of the stock, being equal to the strike. This is more natural as the strike versus stock comparison is only done at maturity, so one should look at forward values of the stock or present values of the strike before comparing and deciding what is ITM or OTM. We can even define a forward intrinsic value that way, which would be $\left(S_0 \exp\left(rT\right) - K\right)^+$ for the call option and $\left(K - S_0 \exp\left(rT\right)\right)^+$ for the put option, where S_0 denotes the current level of the stock.

For convenience, however, we will almost always use the first, which is not uncommon practice in equity markets. The other definitions requiring a calculation to see if an option is ITM or OTM are more common in, for example, FX markets.

1.8.2   Time Value and Extrinsic Value

A concept which is very simple and intricate at the same time is the concept of time value. It is defined as the value of the option 'above' the intrinsic value. At first sight, one might assume that this has to be a positive number, because it is easy to realise that if options are OTM the intrinsic is zero, but the premium one has to pay to be in the market is typically not zero. So the differential is positive and it might be tempting to assume this differential is always positive. In fact, depending on which definition of intrinsic value is taken, the time value will behave differently.

Throughout the book we will use the simple definition of intrinsic value

$$\pi\left(S(t), t\right) - \pi\left(S(t), T\right)$$

and in this case we will see that there are situations where the time value is negative, although most often it will be positive. The time value is also known as extrinsic value.

For stocks without dividend payments the time value is always positive (unless the interest rate goes negative, which we will exclude) [89]. However, as soon as we throw in some complexity, such as dividend payments, time value can become negative as well. This is in fact exactly why there is no difference in premium between an American call option and a European one in absence of dividends [49]. Before moving to the put option, we will prove the positive attitude of the time on a call option.

There is more than one way to prove this result. We will do this by showing how to exercise and capture the intrinsic value of a call option. Suppose we own a call option that is ITM (the other case is trivial since the premium is always positive and hence it is always more than the intrinsic value, being the worthless component of the equation). Since it is a European option, we cannot exercise it straight away as the instrument only allows us to exercise at the maturity of the option. We will use the same notation as before. The premium or value of the option is π_C, the strike is K and the maturity is T, whereas the current value of the stock is denoted by $S_0 = S(t_0)$.

Suppose we want to lock in the intrinsic value $S_0 - K$. The strategy we can follow is to sell forward the stock. This freezes the price risk we have. We know from (1.2) that the forward price of the stock is given by $S(t_0)\exp(r(T - t_0))$. What happens at maturity? There are two outcomes: either the stock value $S(T)$ is above the strike K, or it is below it.

1. If the option ends up ITM, the trader will exercise his option and his cashflows will be

$$\underbrace{(S(T) - K)}_{\text{exercise option}} + \underbrace{\left(-S(T) + S(t_0)\exp(r(T - t_0))\right)}_{\text{forward sell stock}} = S(t_0)\exp(r(T - t_0)) - K.$$

2. In the other outcome, the trader won't exercise and the only cashflow he will see is the one of the forward sell. But in this case we know that $S(T) < K$, so we get as a cashflow

$$\underbrace{\left(-S(T) + S(t_0)\exp(r(T - t_0))\right)}_{\text{forward sell stock}} > S(t_0)\exp(r(T - t_0)) - K.$$

Now, since for positive interest rates this outcome is always bigger than $S(t_0) - K$, we see that holding the option and hedging it by forward selling the stock gives a total value above the intrinsic. Clearly this means that the cost of this hedge needs to be above this final guaranteed outcome, or $\pi_C > S(t_0) - K$. In fact the construction ensured that the premium is even above the forward intrinsic value: $\pi_C \geq S(t_0)\exp(r(T - t_0)) - K$.

EXERCISE 1

Why does this argument go wrong when there are dividend payments in between?

We can wonder why this argument does not hold for put options. It looks perfectly reasonable to do the same thing. For hedging this instrument (again only when it is ITM), we need to buy forward a stock. Following the exact same lines of thought, we can show that the premium should be bigger than the forward intrinsic value: $\pi_P > K - S(t_0)\exp(r(T - t_0))$. However, it is now clear that since $K - S(t_0)\exp(r(T - t_0)) < K - S(t_0)$, it becomes possible that the premium π_P is less than the intrinsic value, at least mathematically.

So the situations where the time value is negative can be traced back to the cashflows. Receiving money now or receiving the same amount of money in the future is not the same. And the direction of the cashflows in case of the put option are reversed (since we forward buy the stock rather than sell, and the moneyness at maturity will be the opposite case).

This whole construction is a nice example of proxy hedging the option [36]. However, the outcome of the hedging strategy is unsure. We had inequalities rather than equalities, which distinguishes the OTM case from the ITM case. In fact, taking one step backwards and gazing at the equations teaches us that the reason for the residual risk has to do with the fundamental aspect of options. We started by saying that the option was ITM and hedging accordingly. If then, afterwards, it turns out to be OTM, there arises a risk or an uncertainty in the value the hedge will produce. The balance between the option and the hedge is broken at that time. The next chapter will reveal in detail how the trader who owns an option should manage his book dynamically in order to reduce or even eliminate the uncertainty compared to the strategy described above.

1.8.3 Being Long, Short or Flat and Neutral

These concepts describe the position of a trader. Being long or having length in the stock means that you own a certain amount of stocks. Being long 200 stocks, means you own 200 stocks (or the delta-equivalent of options which will be explained in Chapters 2 and 3). Clearly this is a favourable position if the stock goes up, and a bad position to be in when the stock value starts declining. Be aware that this is terminology used for a position, rather than a single transaction. If a trader is long 200 and sells 50, he is still long 150.

A short position corresponds to the opposite position, where the trader sold more stocks than he held. For individual investors this is not always allowed, but professional traders are allowed to do this. During the credit crunch crisis, there were restrictions imposed by the regulators [9] on having short positions, as it was argued that speculators were pushing the markets down by taking exuberantly large short positions in certain bank stocks. However, for an option trader who is delta hedging we will see that he naturally ends up in short positions from time to time.

By entering into options positions, we now know there is a delta-equivalent position in the stocks. For example, the holder of a put option has a short position because of the negative delta a put induces. This position is only favourable if the stock is going down.

The position in between is called flat or neutral. This is almost as if the trader is not influenced by the market. However, in Chapter 3 we will see that although a option trader can start in a neutral position, he can see himself end up in a non-flat position without doing a single transaction. This is one of the aspects of options trading.

1.8.4 Mark-to-Market

Mark-to-market is also known as fair-value accounting. This is the concept we will be using throughout the book and we will abbreviate it as MtM. It means that every instrument in the book is assigned a value that corresponds to the current fair value. If there were no slippage or transaction costs, this would also be the value at which you can clear your position. It is common practice to value a book based on this principle. However, in reality if we buy and then immediately sell a stock, we typically don't get the same price back that we paid. This is what traders refer to as slippage.

For instruments with big liquidity risks (products that, once bought, cannot be sold easily), one might want to keep liquidity reserves. The reason for this is that although we value a position in a stock at the current (mid) market level, the size of the position might not be liquidated at this level. This brings in some more subjective views on the MtM. In Section 4.2 we will come back to this problem in the context of how we can adjust the option values if the bid-offer spread or slippage is large.

1.8.5   Mark-to-Model

Very interestingly, for instruments without a transparent market, such as all exotic options or far ITM or OTM options, one has to depend on a model to valuate them. There is no other reference available and there is a substantial model risk involved. By using the Black–Scholes valuation and our own assessment of the volatility, one is in effect exposed to model risks as well. If, however, the option market by itself is liquid and quotes are available for those instruments, the valuation shifts to the MtM.

1.8.6   P&L

The income or profit and loss (P&L) statement indicates the net income of the operations. Typically, the reported P&L are gross numbers that don't take into account operating expenses or taxes. The daily P&L are the daily changes in the MtM of the entire book, cashflows and interest accounts included. Suppose we are long 100 stocks. If the stock price goes down by 0.75 from one day to the next, our book value will lose $100 \cdot 0.75 = 75$. Traders will say that the P&L is (negative) -75.

In this book, we will assume all stocks, bank accounts and derivatives are in the same currencies. In a trading book in a bank or hedge fund, there will typically be multiple currencies that need to be managed. The P&L of one individual book can be comprised of multiple currencies and for trading companies the funding rate given from the company to the desk or shareholder's view determines the currency that the P&L is expressed in.

Risks are typically followed up very tightly in banks and trading houses, so the daily publication of the P&L is an important risk metric that allows for transparency in what is going on in the books, something that is particularly important when dealing with derivatives.

2 Delta Hedging in the Perfect World

2.1 Some of the Aspects of Volatility

There are many ways to look at volatility, and people working in the industry are so used to this concept that it gets used in different contexts, which is sometimes confusing at first sight to new entrants. Throughout this book, we will keep coming back to this concept and, by breaking it down to its basics, the different points of view will all be clarified.

Let us start by the intuitive meaning of the word, being that volatility measures or represents – in some way or another – the level of fluctuations [69] for a particular price. The way we measure it, the unit we use, the time-scale at which we are looking, all have an impact and should be specified in order to transform a single volatility number into a solid understanding of how much level of fluctuation there is in that particular stock. This points to the understanding that there is a certain amount of convention coming into play. For example, when people announce a certain number for the volatility, it will always be a percentage number and the time horizon is always one year, unless mentioned differently.

By taking a more academic approach based on statistics, one can argue that the value of the stock in one year is uncertain and assign a probability distribution to it [115, 106]. It could be desirable to use the width or standard deviation of this distribution to link to the volatility of the stock. This point of view, as we will explain in a little more detail below, is exactly what has become the market standard.

Before we move into the details, let us take another step down this path that sometimes causes confusion between practitioners and academics. It is clear that the statistical approach is focused on the one-year horizon, whereas a trader, who wants to delta hedge on a daily basis, is not so interested in knowing the uncertainty accumulated over the year. What he is really interested in, is to understand how the uncertainty plays a role on a much smaller scale, such that piled up over the year it leads to the same distribution as the statistician has presented.

In mathematical terms, knowing the distribution at one time (or multiple times) is not enough to complete the dynamic picture. One needs to know how the distribution changes over time [43]. Clearly, on a very short time-scale, let's say one second, the uncertainty is very small and the distribution function should be sharply peaked around the current level of the stock. As the time horizon increases, the density should widen up as depicted in Figure 2.1. In Chapter 1 we presented the dynamic stochastic differential equation describing a model for the movement of the stock. One can show that at any time t, the solution (1.9) to this equation is a random variable $S(t)$ that behaves according to a lognormal distribution [120]. So, at any given time t, we have a density that depends on the original parameters in the equation, being the drift μ and

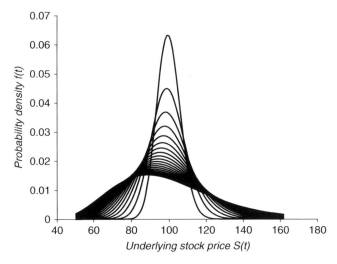

Figure 2.1 For the short-term horizon, the density function is peaked around the current level of the stock price. As we look further into the future, the distribution widens up and more uncertainty gets introduced around the value of the stock price.

the volatility parameter σ:

$$f(s, t; t_0, \mu, \sigma) = \frac{1}{\sqrt{2\pi (t - t_0)}\sigma s} \exp\left[-\frac{\left(\log s/S(t_0) - \mu (t - t_0)\right)^2}{2\sigma^2 (t - t_0)}\right]. \qquad (2.1)$$

As mentioned in Section 1.6.3, option prices can then be calculated as expectations under this density function [133]. For example, the value of a call option is given by the discounted expected value of the payout under this density

$$\pi_C (S(t_0), t_0; K, T) = \exp(-r(T - t_0)) \cdot \int_0^\infty \max(0, s - K) \cdot f\left(s, T; t_0, \mu, \sigma\right) ds \quad (2.2)$$

$$= \exp(-r(T - t_0)) \cdot \int_K^\infty (s - K) \cdot f\left(s; T; t_0, \mu; \sigma\right) ds. \qquad (2.3)$$

This brings us formally to the mathematical or academic way of looking at the volatility. It is *not* the standard deviation of this distribution, but it does control the wideness of the distribution. The first moments are given by

$$E[S(t)] = S(t_0)\exp\left(\left(\mu + \tfrac{1}{2}\sigma^2\right)(t - t_0)\right)$$
$$Var[S(t)] = (S(t_0))^2 \left(\exp\left(\sigma^2 (t - t_0)\right) - 1\right)\exp\left(\left(2\mu + \sigma^2\right)(t - t_0)\right)$$
$$E\left[\log S(t)\right] = \ln S(t_0) + \mu (t - t_0)$$
$$Var\left[\log S(t)\right] = \sigma^2 (t - t_0).$$

For the more technical reader, these are the moments in the original measure, called the historical measure [16], not in the risk-neutral pricing measure. From the previous chapter, it should be recalled that the actual likelihood of direction, or the drift, did not come into play in the binomial tree model. It is also absent from the Black–Scholes formula. Practically speaking, the difference is best seen in the fact that the average future stock price is not identical to the current level but given by the forward price (1.3).

Clearly, if we used another model for the stock price, it would lead to another family of density functions [39], and to other formulas for the moments. In Section 2.2, we comment on the strengths and weaknesses of this particular model.

In a way, when people use the word volatility, they agree, not just on the time horizon and the unit of the number, but on the underlying mathematical model. So, the dynamic statistical approach that was started by Black and Scholes in the 70s [113, 18] unified the way of communicating around volatility. In this book, we will distinguish between historical volatility, implied volatility, realised volatility, instantaneous volatility and imposed volatility. All of these concepts will be explained in Section 2.3.

2.2 Flaws and Vigours of the Black–Scholes Model

Let us make a small detour and try and see why the model that was presented by Black and Scholes stood the test of time [78] despite the many assumptions the model is based on. Although many improvements that deal with one or more of the deficiencies have been presented in the academic literature [2, 4, 29, 12, 23, 72, 85, 98, 101, 143], the BS model remains a popular industry standard. There are many aspects to its success. Some say it was the fact that it was the first model introduced into the market that made all the difference, but in fact this is not entirely true. There was another model introduced earlier [139, 51, 114, 76], which was modelled the stock price as a Brownian motion, rather than a geometric (exponential of) Brownian motion. The major drawback of this earlier model was that there was no mathematical prevention of prices becoming negative. Fluctuations or the volatility parameter within that model would be measured in the same unit of the stock, but as the stock price went down these fluctuations were too large compared to the decreased value and could drive the price to negative numbers.

Black and Scholes [18] modified this model and used a relative volatility, which explains the percentage unit used to express the volatility. As a consequence it becomes much easier to compare the volatilities of two stocks if their prices are in a different unit, or range of values. If one stock is quoting around 100 euro and the other around 5 euro, saying that both of them have a daily fluctuation of 1 euro does not say that much. Clearly 1 euro is a lot if the value of the stock is only around 5 euro. Therefore using relative numbers brings more intuition immediately.

Both models, however, are based on Brownian motion and hence carry characteristics of the normal distribution. This distribution is one of the most wide-spread in the literature, with applications from geology, physics, biology, psychology, and so on [115, 140], it almost feels natural to use it for finance as well. The fact that people are acquainted with its properties certainly helped with getting it accepted in the industry. However, as we saw before, within this model it becomes possible to hedge your risks and to set up your dynamic replicating strategy [141] that allows you to service your client without being exposed to any risk. This is a slight exaggeration of the truth, but we will come back to this later.

Moreover, as we saw clearly in the binomial tree model (but the same holds for the Black–Scholes model), there is no ambiguity around the pricing of options. There is only one way, and that is intertwined with the cost of hedging [1]. Moreover, it even leads to a closed formula solution that allows you to calculate the price of an option in an instant. The time of introduction of the formula coincides with the start of the computer era, and having such a closed formula available allowed for the valuation of thousands of deals within a few seconds. Even now, this closed formula remains one of the key strengths of the model. Some more complicated models lose this feature and one needs to turn to numerical or quasi-closed formulas which introduce numerical problems in the valuation [93, 70, 10, 95]. These more exotic models can be made tractable as well, albeit it requires more attention and effort [154, 84, 104].

Another strength can be revealed by looking at the input parameters in the Black–Scholes formula. There are some contract dependent features such as the strike and the maturity. Next to that there are market parameters that are quite visible in the market, such as the level of the stock and the interest rate. That leaves us with only one parameter, which is σ, the volatility parameter in the Black–Scholes model. Once this is set, the option price is fixed as well. We could also invert this thought by saying that once the option price is fixed, the parameter σ is fixed. We will come back to this, but it is clear that the one-to-one link between the market of options and the volatility parameter establishes a new way of quoting option premiums. Rather than saying that the price of an option is 5 euro, one could say it is 20 per cent volatility in the Black–Scholes formula.

The advantage of doing this would be that again absolute numbers don't bring as much insight. Comparing euro premiums to each other is useless, unless you also specify the other parameters. If you decrease the strike, a call option becomes more expensive, although the underlying volatility of the stock is in theory unchanged. We will see in Chapter 8 that the market's view on this particular issue is different, but we will reserve this for later. Over the years, option traders have developed their own slang, and if you asked them where the market is, you wouldn't get an answer in terms of the stocks they are following, but rather on the levels of volatility that are currently observable [150, 151].

And although this parameter started its life as a number in a mathematical model, it has by now moved through puberty into a young adult's life where it is showing much more mature behaviour. In fact, volatility has become an observable quantity through the market of options and the Black–Scholes formula.

Financial markets have been around for a long time and reliable data sources are available dating back far enough to assess how valid the assumption of the lognormality is. It turns out to be a bad match for reality [133, 25]. For example, the independent increments in Brownian motion lead to the property that all non-overlapping periods are independent as far as the returns of the stock are concerned. So, if you have a return of 5 per cent on one day, this has no meaning at all for the return of the next day. Furthermore, it assumes that the volatility parameter does not change over time as σ is a constant in the model.

However, what is very well known to traders is that there are compensating effects in the market. After a big positive return, market participants might try to lock their profit, pushing the price down the very next day. After a big drop or a crash, people in the market get very nervous and the trading activity goes up, resulting in more

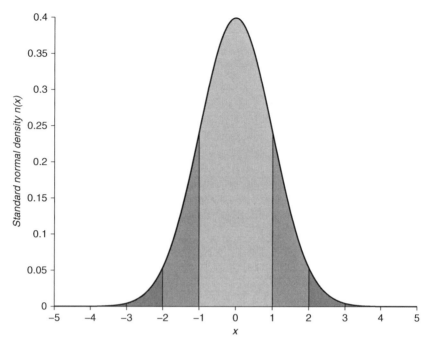

Figure 2.2 The area under the standard normal density function indicates the probability of a $1\sigma, 2\sigma, 3\sigma, \ldots$ move.

volatility over the next days or weeks. These effects are completely neglected by the Black–Scholes model.

The other assumption of normally distributed returns would mean that returns would be in between $-\sigma$ and $+\sigma$ with 68.269 per cent probability. This means that you would have an exceedance of roughly once every three days. This move is called a 1 sigma move. In Figure 2.2 the probability of such a move can be calculated as the integral over the density function of the standard normal distribution over the relevant intervals.

The Table below tells us how often you would have a 2 sigma move or higher.

σ	probability	exceedance frequency	Empirical probability S&P 500 (2008–13)
1σ	68.269%	once in three days	81.79%
2σ	95.450%	once per month	94.64%
3σ	99.730%	once per year	98.08%
4σ	99.994%	once per century	99.21%

When looking at the S&P 500 data in the period between 2008 and 2013, one can observe that the higher sigma moves occur a lot more frequently. For example we had 29 occurrences of a 3 sigma move in these six years of data whereas the Black–Scholes model predicts only one each year. Even more striking is that there were 12 occurrences of a 4 sigma move, which should only occur once every century. As a consequence the probability of being within a 1 sigma radius is a lot lower empirically.

If this is such an unrealistic model, why has it become a market standard? Is it really just because of the advantages that are outlined above? Or is there more to it? Yes, there is more magic to it that this. Throughout the book, we will introduce the reader to the hedging of options, and it will become clear that the Black–Scholes model does a great job at this, no matter how deep its statistical flaws are [78].

2.3   Flavours of Volatility

We already announced the different types of volatility. Some of them are actually wide-spread concepts, some of them we will just use within the scope of this book. All of them will be presented here and they will be used later on in the book.

2.3.1   Realised Volatility

This is probably the most common volatility measure there is. One could imagine selecting a particular stock and a certain time period from the past, and trying to estimate the σ parameter in the Black–Scholes model based on this data. In order to do this, we would require knowledge again of Itô's formula, which allows us to transform the Black–Scholes equation (1.8) into a more suitable format. As we explained before, the whole solution of this equation is following a lognormal distribution. It therefore makes sense to have a look at the logarithmic of the stock price, as this will follow a normal distribution.

So in particular $\log S(t)$ follows a normal distribution. By applying Itô's lemma we can actually write down the dynamic equation this quantity follows [17]:

$$d\log S(t) = \left(\mu - \frac{1}{2}\sigma^2\right) dt + \sigma\, dW(t). \qquad (2.4)$$

The reader who is not familiar with stochastic calculus might find this magic, but if he is willing to take our word for this he might as well observe that this equation is saying that the change in the logarithmic stock price ($d\log S(t)$) is composed of two parts. The drift term is proportional to the period of time over which we observe this change (dt) and the other is determined by noise (Brownian motion) and called the volatility term.

If one wants to estimate the σ parameter of the original stock, one can use lognormal returns over one day and calculate the standard deviation from them. This would give us the volatility over one day, which mathematically speaking is $\sigma\sqrt{dt}$. This follows from one of the properties of the Brownian motion that tells us that the variance of $W(t)$ is given by the time t. That just leaves us with the normalising effect to withdraw the value of σ.

There are several ways to do this however, showing that practice sometimes raises more questions than could be anticipated. The question in this particular case is how many days there are in a year. This might seem an obvious question and you would answer 365. Of course, that would already leave out the leap years. Second, it is obvious that in your dataset, there are no quotes for Saturdays, Sundays or holidays. So, there is no volatility to be observed there. Therefore a common approach is to use the number of trading days in a year, which is in the range of 250 to 255, depending on the particular year and market.

Note that very often people work with the return rather than the logreturn and in fact for daily observations the difference can be neglected:

$$\log\left(S(t+\Delta t)/S(t)\right) \approx \frac{S(t+\Delta t) - S(t)}{S(t)} \text{ for } \Delta t \text{ given as 1 day}$$

but it is good practice to implement the formulas as logreturns as they are also valid if we use larger time steps.

A fair challenge would be to ask if there is really no volatility during the weekend, or if it is just not observed. In other words, is it fair to regard the return from Friday to Monday in the same manner as from Monday to Tuesday? Wouldn't that imply that the world stops turning in the weekend? For that matter, filtering techniques are sometimes applied to estimate the volatility parameter.

Another question to ask is what would happen with your estimate of σ if you used weekly returns, rather than daily, or if you observed hourly data? There have been many papers written on this subject [11, 6, 15] and we can reveal that it *does* make a difference what you use. Typically, the longer the time period, the more normal the returns tend to be. The reason for this brings us back to the last flaw of the Black–Scholes model, as the different hours, for example, are correlated in terms of returns, in contrast to what Black–Scholes prescribe in their model.

Example 2 *In Figure 2.3 we can see the value of the S&P 500 index during a turbulent time period. It is clear that the volatility was a lot higher initially and then reduced a little*

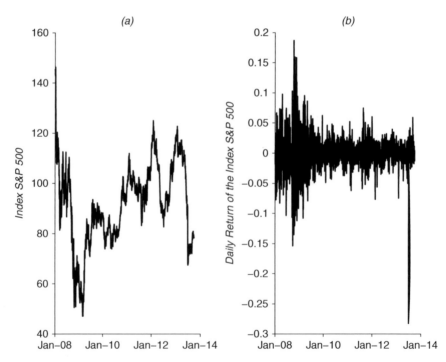

Figure 2.3   (a) The price path of the S&P 500 over the period 1 Jan 2008 until 1 Oct 2013 and (b) the corresponding daily returns over the same time period.

bit over time again. Note the very negative spike down at the end of June 2013. These kinds of returns are huge outliers in the Black–Scholes model but not uncommon in prices of real financial instruments. By calculating the standard deviation over the returns in 2.3(b), we can find

$$std = 2.91\%$$

for the daily volatility. In this dataset we have 2100 calendar days (between 1 Jan 2008 and 1 Oct 2013) out of which 1448 were a day for which there was a price listed. This means we have a ratio of 68.95 per cent of trading days versus calendar days in our dataset. Applying this forward looking, we can assume $365 \cdot 0.6895 = 251.68$ trading days in a year. Using this factor we can then find the annualised realised volatility for the S&P 500 over this period of time

$$\sigma_{annualised} = 46.17\%.$$

2.3.2 Historical Volatility

The next volatility concept up for discussion is what we will refer to as the historical volatility. Very often historical and realised volatility have the same meaning, but we will assign a different definition to it. Once a stock is selected, one can select a *future* time period. The realised volatility that we will observe over this future period is not known at that time (otherwise it wouldn't be the future). We will refer to that volatility as the historical volatility. This is actually the value that should be entered into the Black–Scholes model as it would provide the best match for the future data and hence for the option price. Of course, there are still the other flaws, but within the model this would be the best practice. From a practical perspective this is, of course, an unknown quantity, and the only reason we make this split is to clarify the difference between various experiments we will conduct.

For the historical volatility, we use a certain time-frame, typically the lifetime of an option, which can range from a couple of days to years. It will always be the time over which the trader will be hedging his position and during which he is exposed to those random fluctuations of the stock.

You could say that historical volatility $\sigma_{hist}(t_0, T)$ is the average volatility over the future. Of course, this does not mean that the volatility has to be constant throughout this period. Clearly in the Black–Scholes model you assume it is, otherwise your volatility parameter σ could not be taken a constant. This brings us to the next concept.

2.3.3 Instantaneous Volatility

If you had a crystal ball and you knew that the historical volatility would be 20 per cent over the next year, it would not mean that over the next days you would observe 20 per cent volatility. It could be that the first months the volatility is much lower, barely touching 10 per cent, whereas during the last period it goes up to 30 per cent.

The instantaneous volatility tells you how much volatility your stock is showing right now. We could make a distinction between instantaneous over the past and the future, just as we did between realised and historical. Although a very interesting concept, this is a purely theoretical one as it is impossible to estimate this quantity in practice and we will therefore not distinguish between them.

One last remark to be made here is that when we talk about average volatility, we actually mean average in the variance space. Suppose we write the instantaneous (future) volatility function as $\sigma_{inst}(t)$, we need it to match the historical volatility. One can show [113, 152] that the matching needs to be done in the variance space:

$$\sigma_{hist}(t_0; T) = \sqrt{\frac{1}{T - t_0} \int_{t_0}^{T} \sigma_{inst}^2(u)\, du} \tag{2.5}$$

where we explicitly denoted the time period of the historical volatility.

2.3.4 Imposed Volatility

The next concept is an artificial one. It will allow us to distinguish between lab experiments, which is of course not possible in the financial markets. You could see the real market as an experiment but, in contrast to real experiments, you cannot redo this. Even if you see the exact same settings as you have seen in the past (supposing all economic indicators would be identical), you can rest assured that the market will behave differently from how it behaved on its last encounter. People learn from the past and adapt.

However, in this book we will do such a thing as setting up experiments. We will sometimes use our Black–Scholes model to generate data that perfectly matches the model. We could for example generate stock prices according to (1.8), making sure our data at least matches the model. The parameter that we then use for σ will be called the imposed volatility. However, one should be aware that although this is as close as we can get to a lab set up, it still introduces deviations. Suppose we generate a year of data (daily observations) with an imposed volatility of 20 per cent. Once the data has been generated, one can try to look back at it and estimate the realised volatility. Because of the finite nature of the dataset, it will deviate slightly from the imposed volatility. However, it will be quite close.

2.3.5 Implied Volatility

Another, more market-related, volatility concept is the implied volatility. This takes everything to the next step, taking into account the options market. Up till now, we only talked about the underlying stock and its behaviour, in particular the fluctuations in the past, present and future. However, it is important to realise that the options market has become a very liquid market with many participants, all with their own views and interests. We will come back to this in more detail when we discuss the dynamics of the volatility surface in Chapter 8. For now, we just want to reveal that despite your estimate for the historical volatility, even if you are right on that, you could try to charge more premium for that particular option than would be reasonable according to the Black–Scholes model, similarly to the argument we made in Section 1.3.

So, by observing the price of the option (for a given strike and given maturity), one can back out the σ parameter one has to push into the formula in order to find that price. As it turns out, the market has adjusted for the shortcomings of the Black–Scholes model and the market-implied distribution is not lognormal anymore.

However, the beauty of the Black–Scholes formula is that you can tune your σ parameter such that you match this market price of the option. Clearly this procedure only makes sense if there are indeed option quotes available in the market. Fortunately for a lot of underlying assets, this is the case.

The following statement captures the truth, the whole truth and nothing but the truth around the implied volatility: implied volatility is the wrong number you put into the wrong formula to get to the right price, a quote that is attributed to Rebonato [125]. Sometimes analysts try to use implied volatility to defer conclusions about market direction. It is very tempting to think that this information is present in the option market, but the motivation for buying an OTM put option does not have to be because the buyer is expecting a decrease in the stock price. If you buy house insurance, it is not because you expect your house to burn down, but you balance the risk versus the insurance premium and decide that it doesn't harm to pay this small premium, just in case. A lot of pension funds are operating in the same way. They massively buy protection against crashes in the form of short-dated OTM put options.

From the trader's point of view, knowing there is a huge interest can bring about two thoughts. First of all, the trader should increase his price because the interest is high. This is the basic feature of supply and demand. Second, if the scale of the orders becomes really big, he might become less comfortable with the risk (as we will see later, not all the risks can be eliminated by hedging) and he might want a bigger risk premium for that. Neither of the above lines of thought are expecting a drop in the value of the stock. This means that the implied volatility does not imply anything for the future [54]. We will elaborate more on this in later chapters.

There are extensive studies on comparing the realised or historical volatility to the implied volatility. Typically there is a risk premium in the implied volatility. For a good analysis, we refer to [137, 82].

2.3.6 Hedging Volatility

A last question one can ask oneself is what volatility to use in the hedging procedure dictated by the Black–Scholes model. It may seem like a stupid question, because it has already been answered by the implied volatility. If you can price a particular option, meaning you have the implied volatility available, it is the straightforward solution to use this value as the volatility to hedge with. However, let us assume you have a crystal ball again and you know that the historical volatility is 20 per cent, but you can negotiate your client into paying an implied volatility of 25 per cent. This means that you are selling the option more expensively than it is really worth. If you don't like the rip-off feeling you get here, you could see this as a risk margin, or a service fee or whatever makes you feel more comfortable.

So, the choice remains, which of the two values do I plug into the dynamic hedging strategy to hedge this sold option? As it turns out, it doesn't make that much of a difference anyway [125]. This brings us to yet another strength of the Black–Scholes model. It turns out that the model is so robust that almost any value will do. We will be exploring this in more detail later on. Most derivatives traders choose to use the implied volatility for consistency reasons.

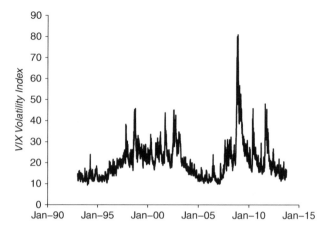

Figure 2.4   The VIX volatility index on the S&P 500 index is a measure for the implied volatility.

2.3.7   VIX, the Volatility Index

The Chicago Board Options Exchange introduced a volatility index, called the VIX [127] (see Figure 2.4), in 1993 that is constructed out of the implied volatilities for short-dated options on the S&P 100 price index. This index, much like the implied volatility, is forward looking by about 30 days. Nowadays people use this as a risk measure and some recent developments even use it as a fear indicator in the market [42].

The initial VIX index was an average over eight different implied volatilities, calculated from eight ATM options with two near term and two next term expiration dates. These option prices were converted into Black–Scholes implied volatilities. In September 2003, the index was refined to better reflect the market-implied volatility and the definition takes into account a wider range of options. In fact, even the underlying index was shifted from the S&P 100 to the larger S&P 500 index and the model dependency was taken out by relying on a particular volatility estimation method. We won't enter into the details of this formula.

2.4   Setting up the Experiment

In order to understand how to manage a book or portfolio of derivatives, we need to start from the basics. We have established by now that the basic toolbox the trader has is the Black–Scholes formalism, containing the Black–Scholes formula to price and the formula for the delta, which tells him how to dynamically hedge his risks. Suppose we put ourselves into a position where we know the underlying stock is following the dynamics that were introduced by Black and Scholes. We could then analyse how the delta hedge procedure works. If this theory is solid, we should be able to eliminate all risks while hedging.

Let us work with an example where the interest rate is fixed at $r = 2\%$. We will take a non-dividend paying stock that will follow a geometric Brownian motion according to (1.8). We will impose a drift of $\mu = 10\%$ and a volatility of $\sigma = 20\%$. Assume the stock has a starting value today of 100 euro. We will generate standard normal deviates

$Z^{(i)}$ and from this we can generate a sample path of the stock [93, 70] by using the solution to (1.8):

$$S(t_{i+1}) = S(t_i) \exp\left[\left(\mu - \frac{1}{2}\sigma^2\right)(t_{i+1} - t_i) + \sigma \sqrt{t_{i+1} - t_i} Z^{(i)}\right] \qquad (2.6)$$

where $(t_i)_{i=0}^N$ is such that $t_0 = 0$ and $t_N = T$, the expiry date. Let us study an ATM call option with a total time to maturity of $\tau(t_0, T) = 0.10$. We will assume the delta-hedging procedure to take place at regular time steps that are $\Delta t = 0.005$ apart from each other. This means that the total hedging takes about 20 steps. All the results are combined in the following table and we will take the reader through the different steps of delta hedging.

Before we dig into the details, let us point out the meaning of the different columns.

1. Step: the step in the delta-hedging procedure. For convenience, we will call each step 'one day'.
2. Z: the random number used for the generation of the stock value.
3. $S(t)$: the value of the stock, starting at 100.
4. Option: the value of the option on each day.
5. Delta: the value of the delta.
6. Stock: the position in the stock as inherited from the previous day.
7. Cash: the cash position inherited from the previous day.
8. Stock BS: the stock position as prescribed by the Black–Scholes hedging model.
9. Cash BS: the cash position as prescribed by the Black–Scholes hedging model.
10. P&L: the profit/loss (P&L) for each day.
11. Total: the accumulated effect of the profit/loss.

Step	Z	S(t)	Option	Delta	Stock	Cash	Stock BS	Cash BS	P&L	Total
1		100.00	2.62	52.52%			52.52	−49.90		0.00
2	−0.0969	99.90	2.50	51.83%	52.47	−49.91	51.78	−49.28	0.06	0.06
3	−0.2337	99.61	2.28	49.82%	51.63	−49.28	49.62	−47.34	0.06	0.13
4	0.5889	100.49	2.67	55.62%	50.06	−47.34	55.89	−53.22	0.04	0.17
5	−0.5743	99.71	2.19	50.23%	55.46	−53.23	50.09	−47.90	0.05	0.22
6	−0.7561	98.69	1.64	42.64%	49.57	−47.90	42.08	−40.44	0.03	0.25
7	0.3756	99.26	1.81	46.49%	42.32	−40.44	46.15	−44.34	0.06	0.31
8	1.1662	100.95	2.63	59.33%	46.94	−44.34	59.89	−57.27	−0.03	0.28
9	−0.0494	100.92	2.52	59.31%	59.88	−57.27	59.86	−57.33	0.08	0.36
10	0.7822	102.08	3.18	68.66%	60.55	−57.34	70.09	−66.90	0.02	0.38
11	−0.6564	101.18	2.51	62.05%	69.47	−66.91	62.78	−60.28	0.05	0.44
12	−0.3337	100.74	2.15	58.58%	62.51	−60.28	59.02	−56.87	0.08	0.52
13	0.0374	100.84	2.10	59.80%	59.07	−56.88	60.30	−58.20	0.09	0.61
14	0.6775	101.85	2.66	70.08%	60.91	−58.21	71.38	−68.72	0.05	0.66
15	1.4363	103.98	4.26	87.72%	72.87	−68.73	91.21	−86.95	−0.12	0.54
16	1.3292	105.99	6.09	96.94%	92.98	−86.96	102.76	−96.67	−0.06	0.47
17	−0.7428	104.93	5.02	95.81%	101.72	−96.68	100.54	−95.52	0.02	0.50
18	−1.6709	102.52	2.75	85.09%	98.23	−95.53	87.24	−84.49	−0.04	0.45
19	1.2704	104.42	4.45	98.55%	88.85	−84.50	102.90	−98.45	−0.10	0.36
20	0.7552	105.58	5.59	99.99%	104.05	−98.46	105.58	−99.98	−0.01	0.35
21	−0.2190	105.30	5.30	100.00%	105.29	−99.99	0.00	0.00	0.00	0.35

Let us explain how the delta-hedging procedure works by going through the table in detail. On the first day, the trader sells the option to a client at a price of 2.62, corresponding to an implied volatility of 20 per cent. Note that this is a fair price, as we know that the volatility we impose onto the stock price is also equal to 20 per cent. So within this experiment the real world drift and volatility are known, hence the entire probability measure is known for the stock.

However, from the time series of the stock we can calculate back the realised volatility after the experiment. This is done by calculating the standard deviation from the logreturns and dividing by the square root of the step size. Doing this we find a realised volatility of only 17 per cent. The reason this deviates from the imposed volatility has to do with the finite size of the dataset. We can already guess that selling the option at the 20 per cent volatility will lead to a gain for the trader. We will come back to this below, where we will lower the transaction price to the realised volatility in this experiment.

After the trader sells the option, he receives his first cashflow: 2.62 euro. For hedging purposes, he will also use 20 per cent volatility. The prescribed delta is given by 52.52%. This means he will have to buy 0.5252 stocks. Note that we will overlook the restriction of a fractional number of stocks for now in order to fully grasp the concept of delta hedging. The trader does this by borrowing money from the bank (or going negative on his cash account). He only needs to borrow 49.90, because of the option premium he got deposited in his account. After these transactions, he has the following instruments in his book: a sold option, with a value of 2.62, a loan with present value 49.90 and a stock portfolio with current value 52.52.

Then we move to the next day, or the next line in the table. The easiest observation is the fact that the outstanding loan is increased because of the interest effect. In this particular case the effect is about 1 cent. The value of the stock has decreased by 10 cents. Because the trader was long the stock, he makes a loss in his portfolio. Because of the delta-position, he loses about 5 cents. However, the option that he sold has also decreased in value. What we can observe is that the option loses more than just 5 cents, bringing the total portfolio at a positive value for the trader. We will come back to this soon, but let us first come full circle.

After the change in the market, and because it is the next day, the value of the delta has changed. The model prescribed that the trader should only hold 0.5183 stocks. So, he will sell part of his stock portfolio at the current levels. With the extra cash that is generated, he pays back part of the loan. This is just a rebalancing of the portfolio and it does not create or destroy any value in the book. It just repositions the trader into a new neutral position to start the next day. This procedure is what is called delta hedging. It is the basis for the management of the options book.

Although the theory of Black–Scholes is prescribing that the hedging cost leads to the option price, we notice a profit coming into the book after just one day of hedging. The reason is that the theory assumes that you are hedging continuously through time, rather than just once a day. That means that the actual move of the stock, although 10 cents after one day, is composed of many more up and down moves before the next day started. If we were able to delta hedge every tick-change of the stock, we would see that the cumulative P&L that is generated would be smaller. So the error is induced by the discrete nature of the hedging strategy [19, 148, 111].

Another way of looking at this is by analysing the actual move of the stock. We see that the random number that was used to generate the value of the second day was $Z = -0.0969$. Clearly this number is a random draw from the standard normal distribution. Although any number is possible in the draw, we can distinguish between small numbers that are concentrated around zero, and numbers coming from a tail draw. This one is clearly a bulk-number. One could say that the volatility of the first day, because of this small draw, is smaller than actually predicted by the distribution. It is smaller than 'the typical number' in a standard normal distribution.

The question one could ask is what random number one has to use in order to see no profit and no loss in this first day. We invite the reader to experiment with the above table and verify that a value $Z = -1.00$, which is exactly one standard deviation out of the mean, does the trick. This brings us to the interesting conclusion that for every day in the delta hedge where the actual move of the stock is less than anticipated, based on the volatility, the trader will have a gain in his book. The reader should indeed verify that by changing to $Z = +1.00$ he again reaches a zero P&L effect for that first day. For every move that is bigger than anticipated, the trader will see a loss in his book.

Because of the statistical nature and the assumed independence of the moves on a daily basis, his losses and gains will average each other out, at least if the volatility that realises corresponds to the pricing volatility at the start. In this example, however, we see that the book does not end at a flat value, but gives a profit of 0.35. As we already explained, this has to do with the fact that the realised volatility is less than 20 per cent. Because there are only 20 steps, the distribution of the random numbers is incomplete and the deviations from the 'regular behaviour' are more substantial.

2.5 Doing More Experiments

There are many more interesting conclusions that can be drawn from analysing the table above. We will formulate those in the form of exercises. Each of these exercises is discussed to make sure that the basics the reader is building in understanding the concept of delta hedging are sound.

EXERCISE 3

Suppose the trader does not delta hedge. What would have been his total P&L at the maturity of the option?

Solution 4. *This is an easy question. He sold the option and collected 2.62 euro on day 1. This would go into the bank account and accrue interest. At maturity $T = 0.10$, the balance would read*

$$2.62 \cdot \exp(0.10 \cdot 0.02) = 2.63.$$

The option has expired ITM so the client will exercise and this will lead to a negative cashflow of $105.30 - 100 = 5.30$ for the trader. The total P&L is then -2.67, which is of the same order of magnitude as the option premium. Had the option been a put option, it would have expired OTM and there would have been no claim at expiry. The trader would have gotten to keep all the premium. Typically, not hedging introduces risks that are much larger than the premium allows for.

EXERCISE 5

Change the pricing volatility to 25 per cent. What is the effect on the total value of the book after the option has expired? What happens if we change this value to 16.77 per cent?

Solution 6. *If we increase the pricing volatility, it is quite clear that we are collecting more premium. Therefore the P&L will get bigger. By running the numbers, one can find that the P&L will be equal to 0.98. If we lower the volatility to 16.77 per cent, we know that the P&L will be lower. As the realised volatility is at this level, one can expect that the P&L will indeed be around zero.*

EXERCISE 7

Change the hedging volatility to 0 per cent. What is your observation on the values of the delta? This procedure is called intrinsic hedging. What is the observation in terms of the total P&L? And what about the individual daily P&L moves?

Solution 8. *When we plug zero into the formula of the delta, we typically get an error as there is a division by zero. One can either mathematically calculate the limit for $\sigma \to 0$ or plug in a very small number like $\sigma = 0.00001\%$. The conclusion in either case will be that for ITM options, the delta will be equal to 1 and for OTM options, the delta will be equal to 0. This means we hedge either the full percentage of the stock, or nothing at all.*

Every time the stock price flips above or below the strike, the delta hedge gets adjusted (and only in those instances). Typically one would observe a pretty big loss when it happens and the P&L will strongly depend on the number of such flips. The whole reason the Black–Scholes model works well in terms of hedging is that the risk is diffused. On days where the delta hedge doesn't change, the P&L for the intrinsic hedging strategy will depend completely on the change in the option price, as the hedge is not really working well.

EXERCISE 9

Change both the hedging volatility and the pricing volatility to 0.0001 per cent. What are the observations in terms of the total P&L and daily P&L moves? When do we observe daily P&L jumps?

Solution 10. *This means the option is given away for free. So there is no premium profit. Of course this is not a good strategy for the trader, but let's assume we are the ones obtaining the option for free. If we hedge intrinsically, we have no premium risk, and if the stock crosses through the strike during the hedging period, we will make money. Of course the outcome of our P&L is completely uncertain as we don't know if and how often this will happen.*

Option books can be influenced, but only for a short period of time. What happens if right after the price agreement has been done, the market volatility drops to 5 per cent? What are the conclusions on the daily and the total P&L?

Solution 12. *This means that the trader will see a nice juicy profit in his book, coming from the difference between just having sold the option at 20 per cent implied volatility versus the new market condition being only around 5 per cent. However, this profit will die out if the trader hedges the option during the lifetime, because the final P&L will depend on how the realised volatility turns out. The smart trader would of course try to buy back this option in the market if possible and hence lock in this margin.*

3 The Balance between Gamma and Theta

3.1 Expanding the Option Price

We will dig into a small bit of theory because it will help us to understand the concept of hedging on a deeper level. For this we will use the Taylor expansion [138]. One can show that any function can be approximated by a polynomial function [103]. The coefficients for this polynomial are determined by the derivatives at a single point (the current market conditions). In general the approximation gets better as we add more terms to it. We will come back to this concept in Chapter 6. Recall that the option price π is a function of the underlying stock S and the time t. Of course the price of the stock depends on the time of observation but for the sake of simplicity of notation we will write S instead of $S(t)$ as the time is already explicitly mentioned in the option price.

For the purposes of this chapter, we will break down the expansion at the second order term in S and the first order term in t, neglecting the cross terms. In the following chapters we will extend the expansion to include more variables, and in Chapter 6 we will add higher order terms. Once we have started to see and appreciate the full depth of hedging, the need to include these higher order terms will become clear.

Denote the current level of the stock as $S_0 = S(t_0)$. The Taylor expansion in its two-dimensional form [7] is given by:

$$\pi(S,t) = \pi(S_0, t_0) + \frac{\partial \pi}{\partial S}(S_0, t_0) \cdot (S - S_0) + \frac{1}{2}\frac{\partial^2 \pi}{\partial S^2}(S_0, t_0) \cdot (S - S_0)^2$$
$$+ \frac{\partial \pi}{\partial t}(S_0, t_0) \cdot (t - t_0). \tag{3.1}$$

For readers less familiar with Taylor approximations, we can point out that a first order approximation means we are approximating the option price with a straight line. The second order approximation means we are using a parabolic shape. In Figure 3.1 we can see that the linear approximation for a call option is always below the price graph due to the convexity of the call option price. The same would hold for a put option. The parabolic approximation is almost indistinguishable unless we move away substantially from the initial level, which in the graph is set at $S(t_0) = 100$. In the expansion (3.1), we already recognise the Δ in the second term. Below we will define the gamma Γ and the theta θ that will allow us to write this expansion in terms of the Greeks. Recall that the delta was always revealing how many stocks we had to buy or sell in order to hedge our position. As we explained in detail in the delta-hedging procedure, however, there are discrete effects [19, 152] playing a role. Up to now, we only had a qualitative understanding of those. The introduction of gamma, Γ, and theta, θ, will help us to quantify them.

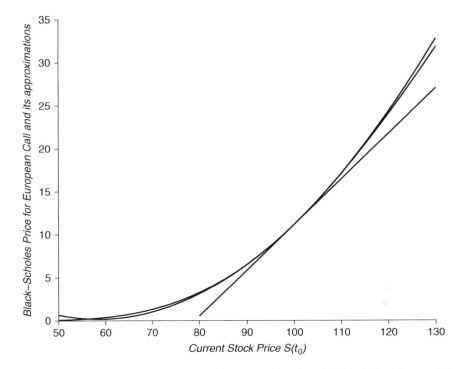

Figure 3.1 The price of a call option, its linear approximation (delta hedge) and a parabolic approximation.

As the purpose of this book is to bring closer theory and practice around option pricing and hedging, we will look at the two new Greeks we introduce in this chapter from several points of view. From a mathematical point of view, the gamma is the second order derivative of the option price with respect to the value of the underlying. Theta is the mathematical derivative with respect to time t. There, we said it once. Let's write it down and get it over with

$$\Gamma = \frac{\partial^2 \pi}{\partial S^2} \text{ and } \theta = \frac{\partial \pi}{\partial t}. \tag{3.2}$$

Note that both these expressions occur in the Taylor expression (3.1). Hence we can rewrite the latter in terms of the Greeks as follows. Denote the current option price as $\pi_0 = \pi\left(S(t_0), t_0\right)$ and write $\Delta S = S - S_0$ as the shift in the stock and $\Delta t = t - t_0$ as the shift in time. We then obtain:

$$\pi\left(S_0 + \Delta S, t_0 + \Delta t\right) = \pi_0 + \Delta \cdot \Delta S + \frac{1}{2}\Gamma \cdot \Delta S^2 + \theta \cdot \Delta t. \tag{3.3}$$

This concludes the theoretical approach. The next sections will focus on sharpening our intuition and understanding of these seemingly very abstract mathematical concepts.

3.2 Defining the Greeks: Gamma

Before we start refining our knowledge, we have to explain why options are called non-linear instruments [75]. This means in layman's terms that when the value of the stock is increasing, the value of the option does not change in a fixed proportional manner. For example, with an interest rate of $r = 2$ per cent, a time to maturity of $T = 1$ year, a volatility $\sigma = 20\%$ and a stock price of $S(t_0) = 50$, an ATM call option is worth 4.46 according to the Black–Scholes formula. If the stock moves up by 1.00, the option moves up by 0.60. However, if the stock moves up by 2.00, the option moves more than double this amount. The following table illustrates this.

Stock price move	−8.00	−4.00	−2.00	−1.00	−0.50	0.00
Call option price move	−3.32	−1.99	−1.08	−0.56	−0.29	0.00
Put option price move	4.68	2.01	0.92	0.44	0.21	0.00
Stock price move	0.00	0.50	1.00	2.00	4.00	8.00
Call option price move	0.00	0.29	0.60	1.23	2.61	5.72
Put option price move	0.00	−0.21	−0.40	−0.77	−1.39	−2.28

So we see that each move in the stock induces a change in the option price, for both the put and the call option. We will focus on the call option first. Notice that the increases in the option prices are themselves increasing as well. So, the rate at which the option price is increasing becomes bigger at each step when we double the stock change. On the downside, we see that the call option decreases less fast than the stock price. For the put option we see the same features, but a put is designed to create value for falling markets (or provide protection against them).

In absolute numbers, however, we see that the changes in the stock are still bigger than the option moves, but besides the non-linear behaviour, they should be regarded in respect of the initial investment. An investment in a stock would be 50.00, whereas the investment in the option would only be 4.46, about 10 per cent of the one in the stock. So when using options, the returns on the investment are much more leveraged with respect to the stock.

EXERCISE 13

Imagine you have an investment budget of 100.00, and the following instruments are available: an OTM call with price $\pi_1 = 1.27$, an ATM call with price $\pi_2 = 4.46$, an ATM put option with price $\pi_3 = 3.47$ and the stock with current price $S(t_0) = 50$. If we know that, within the same day, the stock is going to rise by 10 percent, which would be the preferred investment?

Solution 14. *Our strategies to choose from are*

- *Buy the stock: we would be able to buy 2 stocks and with a return of 10 per cent, we would make 10 euro on this strategy.*
- *Buy the ATM call option: we would be able to buy 22 call options. Each of those call options would rise to 7.80 euro, giving us a total profit of 73.48 or more than 73 per cent return on investment.*

- Buy the OTM call option: we would be able to buy 78 of those and the profit per option would be 1.60 per option, leading to a profit of 124.61 or more than 124 per cent.
- Buying a put option is pretty useless, since it would move in the opposite direction. But of course, we could consider selling put options if our risk department would let us.

EXERCISE 15

Given the same situation as Exercise 13, suppose you are not subjected to budget limits, but rather to volume limits in the sense that you can only buy one financial instrument.

Solution 16. *It depends on how the volume limits are set, but typically one would measure an option either by its delta or by 1 (if the risk limits are set strictly). In the latter case, the call option strategy would only provide you with $2 \cdot (7.80 - 4.46) = 6.68$ euro while the stock strategy would give you 10 euro profit.*

If the volume restriction is set by the delta, the difference between the two strategies is marginal (the option would still win because of the gamma, as we will explain later on).

Now that we understand that the option price moves with the stock changes, it is very instructive to bring the delta hedge back into the picture. We can calculate that within the same settings as above, the delta for a call option is given by $\Delta = 57.93\%$. This means that for every call option, we need to hedge 0.5793 stocks. In consequence, if the stock then moves 0.50 up, the monetary change in our book as far as the stock is concerned is given by $0.5793 \times 0.50 = 0.29$. If we compare this to the change in the call option in the upward move, we see the same result arising. Note also that the -0.50 move (down move) could have been explained by this. In other words, the option movement is perfectly replicated by holding this number of stocks.

We can make almost the same observation for the put option. In this case the delta is given by $\Delta = -42.07\%$. This means that for every put sold, one needs to sell (because of the minus sign in the delta) 0.4207 stocks. If the stock moves by 0.50, the hedge moves $0.4207 \times 0.50 = 0.21$, perfectly corresponding to the change in the put price. We can conclude that changes in both the put and the call option can be perfectly replicated by holding the correct number of stocks. This is good news as it confirms that the delta hedge works.

The non-linear effect only kicks in for movements that are bigger. For this purpose, consider the following table, which contains the move in the stock and the effect on the hedge by holding the appropriate amount of stocks.

Stock price move	−8.00	−4.00	−2.00	−1.00	−0.50	0.00
Call option hegde move	−4.63	−2.32	−1.16	−0.58	−0.29	0.00
Difference option-hedge	**1.31**	**0.33**	**0.08**	**0.02**	**0.00**	**0.00**
Put option hedge move	3.37	1.68	0.84	0.42	0.21	0.00
Difference option-hedge	**1.31**	**0.33**	**0.08**	**0.02**	**0.00**	**0.00**
Stock price move	0.00	0.50	1.00	2.00	4.00	8.00
Call option hedge move	0.00	0.29	0.58	1.16	2.32	4.63
Difference option-hedge	**0.00**	**0.00**	**0.02**	**0.07**	**0.29**	**1.09**
Put option hegde move	0.00	−0.21	−0.42	−0.84	−1.68	−3.37
Difference option-hedge	**0.00**	**0.00**	**0.02**	**0.07**	**0.29**	**1.09**

Several conclusions can be drawn from analysing this table. First of all, we see that the difference between the hedges is very small up to changes in the stock of about 2.00 euro (or 4 per cent). In fact one can easily check, using a simple spreadsheet and the implementation of the Black–Scholes formula, that the difference between the hedge and the option is indeed less than 0.01 up till movements of 0.50 in the stock. This corresponds to changes of the order of 1 per cent of the value of the stock.

Note that a daily or instantaneous change of 1 per cent can be annualised using the same procedure as we discussed in Section 2.3.1 for the volatility. We just need to multiply by the square root of the number of days in a year. Suppose we multiply by $\sqrt{365}$, we see that the 1 per cent daily move more or less corresponds to an annual uncertainty of 20 per cent, which is exactly the implied volatility. So, we have come full circle in showing that we are indeed hedging well as long as the actual move is smaller than the one predicted by the implied volatility (or to be more accurate by the hedging volatility).

Another observation is that apparently the hedging for the put and for the call is equally good. Glancing at those numbers, the reader should guess this level of correspondence cannot be a coincidence. In fact it is not. It has to do with the put–call parity we discussed in Section 1.7. From that relation, we know that the delta of a call is related to the delta of a put, or

$$\Delta_C - \Delta_P = 1. \tag{3.4}$$

One consequence is that the deviation from the delta hedge once the stock starts moving behaves the same for the call and the put. This means that the cost of hedging of a call and a put will be the same.

By looking at the hedging error in Figure 3.2, we see a remarkable effect, namely that it seems to grow more or less quadratically with the move the stock makes. Looking at this from the trader's point of view, it is not hard to realise that the curvature of this parabolic shape determines how good his hedge is for this particular option (or more accurately stated how robust the hedge is once the stock starts moving). It brings about an interesting perspective. Suppose the trader bought the option from a client and he set up the hedge to manage his risk that he inherited from this transaction. Let's focus on an example: the trader bought the ATM call option and sold Δ stocks in his delta-hedging procedure.

Suppose the stock then moves up by 4.00 euro. We can read from the table above that the trader has a gain of 0.29 on his total position. Of course the reason can be found in the fact that he waited too long to rebalance his portfolio. But from his point of view, it is interesting to realise that he is making extra money (besides the margin he might have charged on the premium). And the bigger the move, the more money he makes. It is important to realise that even for drops of the stock, the trader is making moneys. At this point, the reader should be startled, puzzled, excited and ready to try and find a job as an option trader. Such a trader can make money without risk it seems, unless of course the stock remains at the exact same level, but this is extremely unlikely.

Let's blow this up even further. We remember from Chapter 2 that the delta-hedging procedure is a dynamic procedure where, at some points in time, we rebalance the portfolio. Suppose that after this upward move of 4.00 euro, the trader decides to rebalance his portfolio. This means in particular that the delta has gone up from a

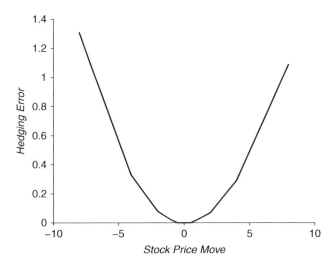

Figure 3.2 The hedging error. The x-axis depicts the move in the underlying stock price and the y-axis gives the P&L between owning the option and selling the hedge for either a put or a call option.

value of 57.93 per cent to 72.07 per cent. So the trader has to sell more stocks, meaning that his cash balance will increase. For now, we will assume that this is all happening within the same day (later we will see that this is a crucial assumption). And suppose for simplicity that interests are not due for intraday transactions.

So, after this rebalancing, he is again in a perfectly hedged position like the one he started with. If the stock then moves down again by 4.00, the option will go back to its original value and original delta. At that point the trader could decide to rebalance again. That would mean he would sell off the extra stocks. As a net result you could say he sells $0.7207 - 0.5793 = 0.1414$ stocks at a value of 54 and buys the same amount back at 50, making a 4 euro profit on this amount. This leads to yet again a profit in his book of 0.57 euro, but not just a MtM profit but an actual cash profit which is fully locked in.

So combined the happy trader has made 0.86 euro in his strategy because he made a profit on his hedge when the stock moved up, he consequently rebalanced and again made a profit when the stock went down. The second profit is of the same kind as the first one because we explained above that, regardless of the direction, there is a positive gain if the trader owns the option and sells the hedge. The delta-hedge strategy makes you sell at the high and buy at the low. Note that this holds for put options as well as for call options.

This does sound like a fun profession. Traders who own options and hedge them make money, and traders who sell options would obviously lose all the time. Before we solve the paradox, we will satisfy our greed (obviously our greed for knowledge) and try to quantify how much of this free money can be made, or in other words what the parabolic shape looks like exactly. From the rebalancing argument we made in the example, it becomes obvious that the change in the delta when the stock moves up and down determines how many stocks the traders can safely buy at a high value and sell again at a low value, and still remain hedged at the rebalancing points. We know that the change in any quantity is measured by the mathematical derivative. So, we need to know the derivative of the delta or $\partial \Delta / \partial S$. We realise that delta was already the mathematical derivative of the option price π with respect to S, telling us how the option price was varying with changing values of the underlying. In summary, the measure that tells the trader how much profit he can generate with fluctuations in the stock value is given by the gamma or $\Gamma = \partial^2 \pi / \partial S^2$.

If we want to be able to predict how much profit this strategy could bring to the trader's book, we need to go back to the Taylor expansion formula (3.3). This formula tells us exactly how accurately an option position is hedged by taking the Δ position in the stock, by searching the Γ term in the approximation, which is exactly measuring (up to second order) the difference between the delta hedge and the change in the option value. This term is called the cash gamma and is given by

$$\Gamma_{P\&L} = \frac{1}{2}\Gamma \cdot (S - S_0)^2. \tag{3.5}$$

From this formula, we do indeed see both ingredients. The faster the option deviates from the hedge, the more profit can be generated from this construction, represented by the Γ factor. Second, the bigger the actual movement, the more profit, but this profit is not generated in a linear way. This quadratic generation of profit is really interesting, because the longer you wait for the stock to move away from its initial position, the better. However, in that case the trader starts taking a risk.

Let's go back to the previous example and let the stock go up. By now we know that this would result in a profit for the trader. However, if he does not react to this and does not buy more stocks as the new delta is prescribing, and the stock consequently moves down again, this profit has disappeared. So the action of not taking action is a risk. But you could argue that it is more of a loss of opportunity type of risk. We will show later on that this is not the correct way of looking at it and that this represents a real risk.

We will conclude this section by stating the exact form of this remarkable Greek in the Black–Scholes world. It is an easy exercise [78] to derive the form of the gamma, being the derivative of the Δ of the call or put:

Gamma Γ		
Γ_C	$\exp\left(-q(T - t_0)\right)$	$\dfrac{\phi(d_1)}{S(t_0)\sigma\sqrt{T - t_0}}$
Γ_P	$\exp\left(-q(T - t_0)\right)$	$\dfrac{\phi(d_1)}{S(t_0)\sigma\sqrt{T - t_0}}$

where ϕ is the density function for the standard normal distribution:

$$\phi(x) = \frac{1}{\sqrt{2\pi}}\exp\left(-\frac{1}{2}x^2\right).$$

Figure 3.3 shows a typical shape for the Gamma Γ for two different maturities as a function of the underlying price $S(t_0)$. The plot is very similar to the bell-shaped normal distribution but the extra $S(t_0)$ factor in the denominator introduces a bit of skew, which was also visible in Figure 3.2.

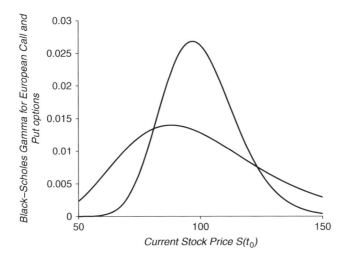

Figure 3.3 The Black–Scholes gamma for a European call and put option is identical. For shorter maturities the gamma is more spiked and for longer-dated options, the profile is more spread out.

3.3 Defining the Greeks: Theta

Clearly the story so far is too good to be true: holding a call or put and dynamically rebalancing gives a profit due to the gamma. Let us now explain where the paradox is coming from. We left out one very important feature, namely the fact that the trader who owned the option and was making free gamma money out of it had to pay the premium to obtain the option in the first place. So the profit he makes afterwards has to make up for this premium payment.

Suppose the strike is fixed at the ATM level. It is clear that the longer the lifetime of the option, the more expensive the option should be, all other market conditions being equal. In the Black–Scholes model, this would be the value of the stock, the interest rate and the volatility. At a later stage, we will introduce more market conditions such as the skew or smile and term structure of the volatility [32]. The intuition is of course that the longer the lifetime, the more time the stock has to move further into the money. Clearly the critical reader might argue that the downside is certainly there as well. The longer the time horizon, the deeper it could move in the OTM range. However, since we cut off the OTM values by not exercising our option, the downside potential is always the same, namely the loss of the initial premium, whereas the upside potential is unlimited, which introduces an asymmetry that underpins the price difference for options with different maturities.

Turning it upside down we know that the value of the option the trader buys at time t_0 becomes worth less and less with every day that passes by. This process is inevitable and if the stock stays exactly at the ATM level, the option will be worth zero at maturity. So little by little the option loses its value. The change in value from one day to the next is called the theta and denoted with the Greek symbol θ. Clearly this number is expected to be negative for both an ATM call and an ATM put option.

We should, however, warn the reader. Thinking back to the negative time value that was possible for put options casts a shadow over the above argument. Why does the argument 'the longer the lifetime, the more value' not hold for ITM put options? That is because we weren't totally honest. There are in fact two factors that play a role. The longer the lifetime the more potential the option has, but also the longer one has to wait before one can cash one's money. In Chapter 2, we showed that it was possible to collect the ITM value for a call option, with only upside potential, but that for a put option this was not possible. However, for a first understanding of how the time value moves, we will focus on cases where we have positive time value.

It is very interesting to understand that throughout the lifetime of the option, the time ticks are the only predictable part of the world [30, 133]. We know that every day, 24 hours have disappeared into history. We also know that time cannot move any faster or slower and once vanished it can never return, no matter how hard we want it to. Let us turn to an example that will unfold the finesse of the Greek that makes you lose.

Take a stock with a current value of $S_0 = 20$. If the interest rate is fixed at $r = 2.5\%$ and it is known that the volatility of the stock is given by $\sigma = 35\%$, one can easily calculate the value of an ATM put option using the Black–Scholes formula. This value is given by 2.50 euro. Suppose there are 250 trading days in a year [89, 88, 128] (we will for now assume the option only loses value on working days). So we could write a fixed loss of 0.01 euro per day in our book. That would make the loss of time-value completely predictable. However, there would be an inconsistency between the market value and the booked value. By accepting a MtM valuation, we have to accept that we only know the theta today (by definition) and we also know all time value will have disappeared when we reach maturity, but we cannot predict how the time value will behave over time.

In fact, the theta exhibits two features. If we look at the value of the option on every single day, fixing the value of the stock at $S_0 = 20$ and taking steps of $\Delta t = 1/250$, one can try to understand how the option loses its value over time. As it turns out, the option loses little value at the start and this process speeds up as maturity approaches. In the table below, the option value is given on specific days. It is clear from the table that at the start the option only loses 2 cents per week. When there are 100 days left till maturity is reached, the loss per week has doubled to 4 cents.

Over the last week, 39 cents are lost. Most remarkable is that the biggest loss is observed on the very last day, where 18 cents are lost over one single day. This is a very important lesson for a trader who bought the option. He should know that the instrument in his book will lose its value, but what he should also remember is that this process is concentrated on the last few months of the option.

Value	Days left	Value	Days left	Value	Days left
2.50	250	1.99	150	1.66	100
2.48	245	1.96	145	1.62	95
2.46	240	1.93	140	1.58	90
2.44	235	1.90	135	1.54	85
1.20	50	0.94	30	0.55	10
1.14	45	0.86	25	0.39	5
1.07	40	0.77	20	0.18	1
1.01	35	0.67	15	0.00	0

The second feature of the theta we would like to discuss is the dependency on the moneyness. The real potential of an option is found in the ATM range, where the difference between a bad investment (investment that expires worthless) and a plain investment in the stock is the biggest. Suppose the following scenario happens: the put option starts ATM and then the stock moves down, making the put option price rise. Although the value increased, the extrinsic value or added value over the intrinsic value is less than for an ATM option. Clearly if the time value is less altogether, there is less value to lose. Let's fix a particular day to see how what the dependency really looks like.

Stock	Value	Discounted intrinsic value	Time value	Days left
16	4.00	3.92	0.08	50
16	3.99	3.92	0.07	45
18	2.37	1.96	0.41	50
18	2.33	1.96	0.37	45
20	1.20	0.00	1.20	50
20	1.14	0.00	1.14	45
22	0.52	0.00	0.52	50
22	0.46	0.00	0.46	45
24	0.19	0.00	0.19	50
24	0.16	0.00	0.16	45

As an example we investigate the same option as before, but with a time to maturity of 50 days. By looking at the table, it becomes clear that the loss of time value over a week is 6 cents when the option is ATM whereas it is much smaller in the ITM and OTM range, where the stock has drifted away from the strike level.

The combined effect takes place because while time passes by, the stock moves away from the current level. In fact one can think of scenarios where the time value actually first decreases, and afterwards increases again. Suppose the trader owns an ATM put option. Let's make this example artificial so we can expand on all the different aspects of the time value. For the first week, the stock does not move and stays at exactly the same level. We know by now that the time value (and the option value) both decrease. After this week, the stock drops by 10 per cent, so we know that the option price increases but completely due to the increase in intrinsic value since the time value itself has gone down after this drop. We know that if the time value is smaller, the daily decrease in time value is lower than before the actual move. So far so good.

But if the stock moves back up to the ATM level, the option value goes down again, but the time value increases, just because ATM options have more time value. Clearly as of then, the daily loss of time value is also more substantial than before this move back up. The relevant question to ask is how all the changes in time value add up. This is the topic of the next section, where we see the theta in relation to the gamma. But for now, we can already argue that over the lifetime the sum of all changes in time value on a daily basis just add up to the option premium of the first day. The reason behind this is nothing else but the fact that an option, whatever happens during the lifetime,

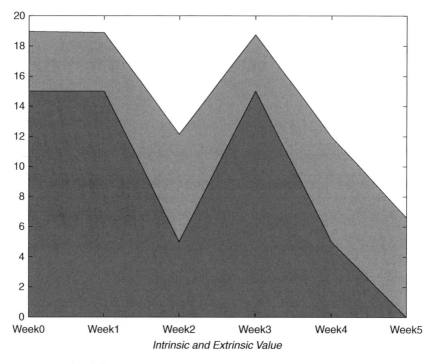

Figure 3.4   A split of the intrinsic and extrinsic value over five weeks in a simple scenario of the underlying stock price $S = 100, 100, 90, 100, 90, 80$ over the various weeks.

converges to its intrinsic value. This observation is in fact quite trivial, but sometimes it is easy to forget the obvious. This behaviour is summarised in Figure 3.4, where a particular path is reflected in a decomposed option value in intrinsic and extrinsic value.

Stated differently, the creation of extra time value is a temporary effect. This can of course lead to decisions to first buy an option and later on sell it before it reaches maturity: trading is born.

We still need to formally define the theta. We already stated the mathematical definition

$$\theta = \frac{\partial \pi}{\partial t}.$$

Interestingly, we can look at the time in two different ways. We can say that if the clock ticks from today to tomorrow, we will have gone to bed, hopefully slept well and the lifetime of the option will be one day less than before. But when working with these partial mathematical derivatives, it is always assumed that the rest of the world does not change. So instead of putting our alarm for the next day, holding our breath and sleeping to make sure the world does not change from one day to the next, except of course the change in time, one could also investigate – with the current market conditions – an option with an expiry of one day earlier. Within the Black–Scholes formalism both approaches are identical [16] due to the Brownian motion being a stationary process and in fact in terms of formulas we can write

$$\theta = -\frac{\partial \pi}{\partial T}.$$

Note that in more advanced models both concepts don't have to coincide, as in some models it is not purely the duration of the option that sets the value, but it might depend on the exact maturity versus the calculation date.

Now both definitions are theoretically valid and useful indeed, but most often in practice we don't look at the theta as the change in the option price over a very small time interval. Very often the practical theta is the change in time value calibrated over one day. There are two ways of approaching this. The first one is using the mathematical definition we had so far. Denote the daily theta with a subscript d:

$$\theta_d = \theta \cdot \Delta t$$

where Δt is one day. As we encountered before, we will need to make a choice on how big a day is exactly. This depends on our day convention. We could say that only business days should be taken into account, meaning that $\Delta = 1/250$ (this depends on the actual year, but usually the number of trading days in a year ranges from 250 to 255 [89]). This means that you stop the time when the weekend arrives. But we already commented that the trading activity might stop over the weekend, but the volatility might not. It is just not visible over the weekend, but on Monday stocks have accumulated news events. So the other extreme is to take 365 days in a year and to take $\Delta = 1/365$ for the transition from a weekday to another weekday, except from Friday to Monday where we take $\Delta = 3/365$.

Now this brings us to the second approach for the theta. We could just say that the theta is the loss in value over one day (to be exact the change in value), and write

$$\theta_d = \pi \left(S_0, t_0 + \Delta t; T, K\right) - \pi \left(S_0, t_0; T, K\right)$$
$$= \pi \left(S_0, t_0; T - \Delta t, K\right) - \pi \left(S_0, t_0; T, K\right).$$

In fact for most practical applications both will give the same numerical outcome because the scope of one day is good enough to use the mathematical derivative approach. If you wanted to know what the theta over a month would be, the second approach would be the one to follow. The mathematical formulation is how academics look at the theta. However, the traders prefer the second approach because it tells them how much the option will have lost by tomorrow. It is more intuitive and, funnily enough, if the question is really how much the option will lose by tomorrow, it is the more accurate one.

The mathematical or academic theta, θ, will be called the instantaneous theta and, if we focus again on the Black–Scholes formula (1.10), we can easily derive the exact formula of the quantity θ [78]:

Theta θ	
θ_C $\exp\left(-r(T - t_0)\right)\left(-\frac{1}{2}F\sigma\phi\left(d_1\right) - rKN(d_2) + qFN(d_1)\right)$	(3.6)
θ_P $\exp\left(-r(T - t_0)\right)\left(-\frac{1}{2}F\sigma\phi\left(d_1\right) + rKN(-d_2) - qFN(-d_1)\right).$	

The θ profile looks like what we see in Figure 3.5. Note that although at first sight the theta is negative, there are two situations where it turns positive. ITM put options are

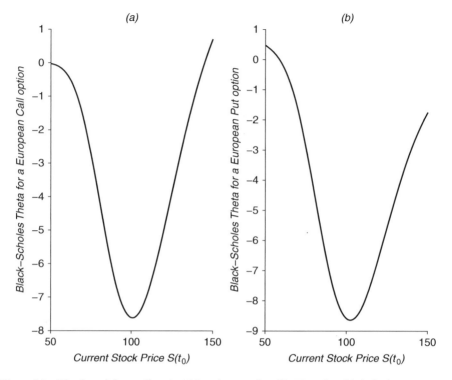

Figure 3.5   The theta θ for a call option (a) and put option (b). Note that this is the instantaneous theta and, as per convention, this usually gets multiplied with $\Delta t = 1/365$ (1 day).

known to have a positive time decay for reasons explained in Section 1.8.2. For ITM options, the theta can turn positive as well, in the case where the dividend yield exceeds the interest rate, and the argument is in fact similar since in this case the forward value (1.3) of the stock is below the current level. In most cases, however, the theta will be negative.

3.4   Gamma and Theta, Always Flirting

Thus far we have seen that an option (usually) loses value over time, because of the theta and because the delta hedging of a long position in an option always brings the trader money. This statement already solves our paradox. There is no free lunch in owning an option. Yes, you will make free gamma money, but you will lose precious theta money. And guess what? There is a balance to be found. A trader that bought an option paid the intrinsic value (if any) and the time value. He knows the time value will be lost during the lifetime of the option. The only thing he does not know is how big the future daily losses/gains will be, but the sum of all these will have to make up for the extrinsic premium paid. He will have to work for his money by actively delta hedging and locking in the gamma profits.

Every single day the trader who owns the option tries to fight the theta by rebalancing his portfolio at appropriate times or leaving the position open if he expects the stock to keep on moving in the same direction. That way he gets to lock even more substantial profits in one single rebalance but, as we explained before, by waiting he is taking a risk. At this point, the market view the trader has kicks in. If he is expecting a rally in the stock or a crash, he might want to wait and have the profit grow. Actually, the option position is helping him make money because of the positive gamma of his book. We say that the trader is gamma long. This is the case for a trader owning one single call or put, but the concept of being gamma long can be extended to a portfolio of derivatives. If the current gamma of the book is positive, we say the trader is gamma long. If it is negative, it is referred to as gamma short.

A position where value is lost from one day to the next is called a theta short position. Two examples we have seen so far are the positions where the trader owns a call option or a put option. Another very simple example is a loan. If you have an outstanding loan, by doing nothing you lose money, namely the interest on the outstanding notional. The opposite position, where you gain money every single day, is called the theta long position. Examples would be the opposite positions as the theta short positions.

Within the Black–Scholes setup, we can derive an expression that exactly specifies this relation between these two Greeks. In fact, verification just requires a little bit of algebra [152]:

$$\theta + \frac{1}{2}(S(t_0)\sigma)^2 \Gamma = r \cdot (\pi - S(t_0) \cdot \Delta). \tag{3.7}$$

This relationship holds for both the call and the put option. One can also show that this relation holds for any portfolio V. The Greeks should then be considered the Greeks of the portfolio. The term π on the right-hand side of the equation should be replaced by the value of the portfolio V [16].

Rather than going through the explicit calculations, we will explain the intuition behind (3.7) below, but let us first investigate some very simple examples.

Example 17 *The most simple example we can apply* (3.7) *to is the stock price itself. Clearly, we can understand that the stock price $S(t)$ has no gamma nor theta and the delta is obviously given by 1. Plugging all those into the relationship we can find π from*

$$0 = r(\pi - S_0)$$

or $\pi = S_0$. So the fair value for a stock is its current level.

Example 18 *Another example we could apply this relationship to is the forward value of a stock. Clearly θ and Γ would still be zero, but the delta in* (1.3) *is given by $\exp[(r - q)(T - t_0)]$, so again $\pi = S_0 \exp[(r - q)(T - t_0)]$, which of course matches out.*

Relation (3.7) is in interesting because it is telling us how all the different Greeks lead to the price. We know that the price of an option, or any derivative in fact, is determined by the cost of hedging. Let's first consider a portfolio of an option that we will delta hedge. The cash part of the portfolio consists of the premium π and the loan with value equal to the value of the stock holdings of the portfolio, which would be $\Delta \cdot S_0$. The interest accumulated over a short time interval Δt on this net amount is given by $r(\pi - S_0\Delta) \cdot \Delta t$. That is the deterministic cost of the construction. On the dynamic hedging procedure we know we will lose the amount of θ. The Γ term requires slightly more attention to explain.

We know from (3.5) that the Γ profit coming into the book would be given by the cash gamma term $\frac{1}{2}\Gamma (\Delta S)^2$. As we discussed in Section 2.3 the volatility σ of a stock measures how big a move we can expect in a time period. Since the volatility is relative, we need to multiply it with the current level of the stock to get to an absolute number. In a certain time interval Δt the typical movement would be $S_0\sigma \sqrt{\Delta t}$, where we recognise the square root term again that keeps popping up whenever we rescale volatility. So the combination of the theta and gamma effect over a time unit Δt is given by $\theta \cdot \Delta t + \frac{1}{2}\Gamma (S_0\sigma)^2 \Delta t$. Putting these pieces together leads to relation (3.7), where we cancelled the length of the time interval on both sides.

In fact this relation reveals the core of the delta-hedging procedure. Gamma and theta constantly need to be balanced in order to make up for the premium and the cost of hedging. Or, reformulated, the premium corresponds to the cost of hedging in a general way, taking into account the loan, the time value change of the book and the expected gamma profit/loss. Understanding this balance is key to understanding how to manage a book of options.

If we rewrite (3.7) back by using the explicit partial derivatives, it reads

$$\frac{\partial \pi}{\partial t} + \frac{1}{2}S^2\sigma^2 \frac{\partial^2 \pi}{\partial S^2} - r\pi + rS \cdot \frac{\partial \pi}{\partial S} = 0. \tag{3.8}$$

This equation [135] is a partial differential equation (PDE) known as the Black–Scholes equation. Its solution is unique when the boundary and initial conditions are set. The boundary condition is given by the payout profile at maturity and the initial conditions are set by the stock price at time t_0. In fact, this PDE is closely related to the heat equation [107] in physics. The link between this PDE and the heat equation is a simple transformation [153].

3.5   How Cute do they Look?

Before even thinking about trading options and delta hedging it is crucial that we know and understand what the Greeks look like. We have seen why they are relevant and how they do their job, but you can't run the job without seeing their features and being able to forecast blindly how they might change when new market conditions develop. A good trader can always anticipate what his Greeks will look like after or during rapid market changes (see the Haug contributions in [150, 151]). We will therefore now investigate the behaviour of the Greeks we saw thus far for both the call option and the put option. The important lesson here is that all the conclusions can easily be drawn by understanding the time value of an option. This by itself will turn out to be enough to qualitatively understand the behaviour of the Greeks. The quantitative understanding requires the expressions provided by the model. In our context that will be the Black–Scholes model and all the formulas we have given the reader up till now, as well as the formulas still to come.

From Figure 3.6 we can read off the value of the call and put option as a function of the level of the stock at different times ranging from a one-year option to the intrinsic

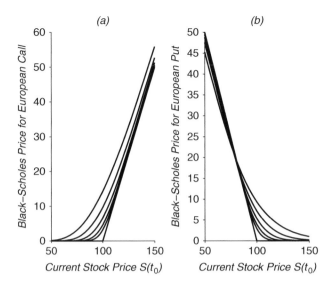

Figure 3.6   The price of a call option (a) and a put option (b) as a function of the current stock price for a variety of maturities (1 year, 6 months, 3 months, 6 weeks, 3 weeks and at maturity).

value (zero maturity), as well as a function of time to maturity. The latter ones are more easily interpreted by looking at them from the right to the left. We took an interest rate of $r = 5\%$, a volatility of $\sigma = 30\%$, a strike of $K = 100$ and the BS formula to generate the graphs. But, in fact, the results that we will discuss below are valid in any model [79].

A lot can be learned from Figure 3.6 and, when analysing the Greeks, we will always come back to this kind of plot. In particular one can see that the larger the maturity, the more smooth the curve looks. As we move through time, we will be going from the smooth curve to the payout profile functions. Sometimes people refer to the intrinsic function as a hockey-stick function because of its resemblance.

Mathematically there is a singularity [63] in this profile, exactly in the strike point, because you change from one regime to another. This singularity becomes visible when we move closer and closer to the maturity date, but far from that date, the function is smooth.

3.5.1 Delta Looks Smart

From the hedging argument, we already know that for OTM options the delta should be close to zero because little hedging is required for these options. In the same spirit ITM options require almost full hedging. This means that the delta is close to $+1$ for call options and close to -1 for put options that are very far ITM. Because of the nature of these values the delta is often expressed in percentages, as it says how much percentage of the actual stock is required to hedge the option. We could expect that exactly halfway, namely at the strike level, the delta should be 0.5 for a call option and -0.5 for a put option. We already explained in Section 1.8.1 that this is not exactly true, but for a qualitative description it will do.

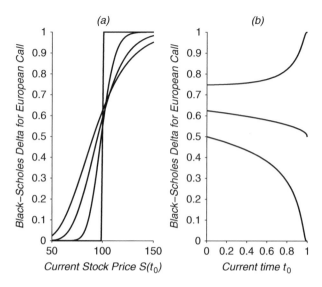

Figure 3.7   (*a*) The call option delta for three different maturities, as compared to the intrinsic delta. (*b*) The delta for an ITM (top), an ATM (middle) and an OTM (bottom) call option as a function of time t_0.

Determining the intrinsic values for the delta is rather easy. For a call option, the intrinsic value is 0 for OTM options and +1 for ITM options. For a put option it is also 0 for the OTM option, and −1 for ITM puts. The intrinsic deltas are valid at maturity when we are actually exercising the option (remember that the intrinsic value corresponds to the value of an option if we would exercise this immediately). Clearly in the context of hedging, it seems a bit silly to investigate the hedging ratio or delta once the option has matured. The reason that we do so anyway is because it helps us understand and memorise the shape of the delta. The reader should remember that at maturity most Greeks have a very pronounced or digital shape.

Once we move ourselves away from maturity, the delta becomes much smoother shaped. The discontinuity in the value disappears, as we see in Figure 3.7(*a*), so the further we are from maturity, the flatter the curve looks. In Section 1.8.1 we discussed that a possible definition of the ATM point would be where the delta is 50 per cent (to be correct we would have to say that the delta is 50 per cent for a call option and −50 per cent for a put option, but in this section we will refer to both values as 50 per cent). However, a closer investigation now reveals that one has to be careful with this definition because it also depends on the maturity. We cannot just pick one maturity and derive the ATM point, since the 50 per cent point would shift towards the strike level as time to maturity becomes smaller.

Figure 3.7(*b*) exhibits the deltas for the three different regimes (OTM, ITM and ATM) as a function of time to maturity. We see that the delta converges faster and faster to its intrinsic value as time to maturity goes to zero. You could say that the option picks its direction. That is true, except for the ATM option, where the delta remains significantly flatter. We still know that the delta at maturity is zero, but even one second before the maturity the option is still in doubt about whether it will expire ITM or OTM. Since it can't pick sides it remains at 50 per cent. In the figure we focused on the delta of a call option, but we know from (3.4) that the delta of a put option is a similar picture, but shifted towards negative values. This can be seen in Figure 1.4(*b*).

The main lesson to be drawn from this is that the main variation from the delta is always located in the ATM range. We can see that the closer we are to maturity, the tighter the range is where the delta changes from small value to full value. Always remember the intrinsic case as the extreme towards which the regular case will converge as the maturity approaches.

3.5.2 Gamma Looks Sexy

We should remember that the delta for the call and put have the same shape. This is of course again a consequence of the put–call parity. Remember from (3.4) we have that $\Delta_P = \Delta_C - 1$, from which we see that the gamma for both instruments is identical. We see that both deltas are increasing with the stock value. This means that the gamma is positive at all times. That is the good news message we already brought, since it means that owning an option brings you gamma long for any value of the underlying stock.

Since most of the change in delta occurs around the ATM point, we know that the gamma should be largest around this point. The delta flattens out in the OTM range and straightens out in the ITM range. This implies that the variation in the delta disappears in both those cases. Hence the gamma, measuring the variation in the delta, is around zero there. The graph of the gamma resembles the bell-shaped curve of the Gaussian or normal distribution. As we explained above, the smart features of the delta sharpen up as the option gets older. What we can expect from the gamma is that the peak level shoots up and the tail parts of the curve relax.

Any option trader that has sold options can tell you how tricky it can get to manage the book near maturity when the stock is around the strike level [152]. The gamma gets so big that the hedging needs to be done very fast. And, as he is the seller, he is gamma short, with a huge gamma position. If the market keeps moving around the strike level, every rebalance will cost the trader money and the amount of theta he has to make up for it is limited. In some cases, in highly volatile markets, it is sometimes better to either fully hedge at once or fully unwind, depending on what you think the market is going to deliver at the maturity of the option. If you are wrong, it will cost you, but rebalancing in a very volatile market can be even more costly, especially due to slippage or bid/offer spreads.

To see how exactly the gamma blows up for an ATM option, we can investigate Figure 3.8(*b*), where we show the gamma for a fixed stock level as a function of time to maturity. It is very clear that the ATM gamma steepens up very fast near maturity. One can see from Figure 3.8(*a*) that the peak of the gamma curve shifts slightly to the right with time. So the highest value is not attained where the stock equals the strike but instead this point depends on the volatility σ, the dividend yield q, the interest rate r and the remaining duration $T - t_0$. In Section 1.8.2 we discussed some alternative definitions of the ATM point and a new definition could be the point where the gamma becomes maximal.

EXERCISE 19

Verify with a numerical example that the point where the gamma Γ is maximal does not correspond to where the delta $\Delta = 50\%$ [79].

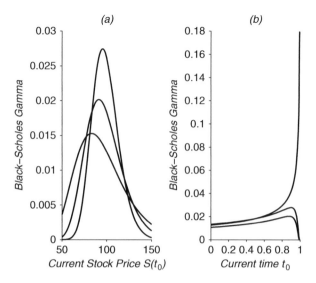

Figure 3.8 (*a*) The gamma for three different maturities. (*b*) The gamma for an ITM (top), an ATM (middle) and an OTM (bottom) option as a function of time t_0.

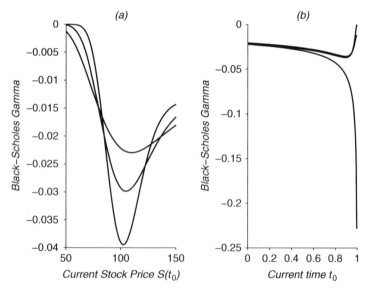

Figure 3.9 (*a*) The call option theta for three different maturities. (*b*) The theta for an ITM (top), an ATM (middle) and an OTM (bottom) call option as a function of time t_0.

3.5.3 Theta Looks Naughty

For the theta we will have to have two sets of graphs, one for the call option (Figure 3.9, where we will assume the dividend yield is zero, $q = 0$) and one for the put option (Figure 3.10).

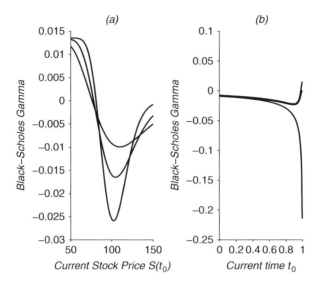

Figure 3.10   (a) The put option theta for three different maturities. (b) The theta for an ITM (top), an ATM (middle) and an OTM (bottom) put option as a function of time t_0.

Now is the time to tie up our loose ends. We have ignored the fact that the time value can be negative, but one glance at Figure 3.6(b) showed that the price of a put option takes a dive below the intrinsic value. We extensively discussed in Section 1.8.2 the possibility that this could happen. We could not ensure for an ITM put that it would be above intrinsic value and clearly from the Black–Scholes results we see that it isn't when stock levels are low compared to the strike.

Correspondingly we see in Figure 3.10 that the theta can be positive for put options. Now what does that mean for the theta-gamma balance that we unveiled throughout this chapter? This means that a trader long the option will gain from both the gamma and the theta, so there is no longer a trade-off, but money is rolling in from everywhere.

Again, a first instinctive reaction would probably be: where is the catch? Well, the sting is in the tail, quite literally here since the premium for these far ITM put options is quite high. So in order to buy this, we need to borrow an amount of cash equal to the premium π. This loan needs to be paid back as well; this cost is high and the payments are due every day in the Black–Scholes model. Again, we can wonder why this argument would not hold for a call option as well. Where did the balance go in the case of the put option? Well, remember that when we own a put option, we need to buy the stock as well to hedge ourselves, so this substantial loan we had just becomes even bigger. For a call they would cancel each other out to some extent whereas for the put the effect gets reinforced.

All very true, but what if we didn't pay that much to the premium? Suppose for example the following scenario. We buy an ATM put option and we start delta hedging it. Suppose the option moves further and further ITM; all of a sudden we find ourselves in the situation where both the theta and gamma are positive. Doesn't that sound like arbitrage?

3.6 Cheating with the Hedging Volatility

In Section 3.2 we saw that the difference between the option and the hedge stayed very small until the stock moved more than was allowed by the prescribed volatility. We might be tempted to think that we could increase the hedging volatility to higher levels so that the hedge stays better for a longer time. This would reduce the amount of work the trader has or, in the case of a gamma short position, would limit the amount of rebalances. In case of a gamma long position, however, if the trader doesn't mind working, he might want to decrease the level of the volatility so that the hedge becomes worse faster, forcing him to rebalance faster.

If we change the hedging volatility, we should also change it in the theta. If we don't do this, we won't be able to see the balance between the two anymore. But that should force us to use the same volatility in the price formula as well. Otherwise we will break the insight we have into the changes of the option value due to the market changes and time. We could cheat even more, though, and use individual volatilities everywhere. However, this would not solve the problem, as any change in volatility in the pricing would immediately be reflected in the pricing and hence in the MtM of the book.

Let us turn to an example to show what happens if we fiddle around with the volatilities. Suppose the trader is gamma short because of an ATM put option with strike $K = 50$, an interest rate of 5 per cent, a lifetime of a year and an historical volatility of $\sigma_{hist} = 25\%$. Let us assume that the option was sold for the BS price, being 3.73. We will discuss the various ways of cheating to see what happens.

Suppose we can change the level in the volatility in both the Greeks and the price. Decreasing the volatility can make it appear as if the deal was very profitable, whereas it wasn't. As soon as the volatilities are decreased, the MtM of the option position does indeed increase, but because of the fact that the realised volatility will be less than the one being assumed after the alteration, we already know that we will see a loss occurring in the book during the lifetime of the option.

So our trading book has advanced to the next level and we will assume the volatility matches the implied or market volatility. But what about the volatility used in the Greeks. We might want to have the hedge as good as possible. Assume we increase the hedging volatility. So during the day, we will feel (false) comfort thinking this hedge is working really well, and the delta does not change so rapidly anymore. Good for us, but of course the valuation does not lie. The valuation is changing and, with a changing stock level, the loss becomes bigger and bigger (remember the position was a gamma short one). For as long as we believe this false hedging volatility, we are blind and we are taking risks without even knowing it.

But wait a minute. Are we really sure about this? Suppose we have an instantaneous volatility function $\sigma(t)$. We already know that the option is priced using an average over this function, but in variance space rather than in volatility space (see (2.5)).

Hedging is a strategy that should protect us from volatility in the stock at this moment. So are we absolutely sure we don't want to use the current value of the instantaneous volatility as hedging volatility? This would be the best protection because the current fluctuations will be of this size, rather than of the average future volatility. We will come back to this question in full detail in Section 7.2.3. For an extensive study and comparison on using the implied volatility versus the historical volatility, we refer to [125].

4

Trading Is the Answer to the Unknown

4.1 Uncertainty and Confusion

In the first part of this book, we focused on the hedging argument of a plain vanilla option. Within the Black–Scholes model, we explained that hedging away the risk can be done quite accurately up to finite-size effect. In real life there are many difficulties [35, 133] that prevent us from believing this model is a perfect representation of the world. However, as we will see later on, these flaws in the model do not take away the valuable lessons we can learn from it [79]. Moreover as it turns out, a solid understanding of the same basic flaws in the model allow a good trader to anticipate and take position in a smart way.

In this chapter we will learn by means of a simple example how trading volatility [118, 119] will work. Before we can start talking about trading, we need to introduce uncertainty and dynamics into the picture. If something is known completely deterministically, there is not much trading around it; it is purely a hedging story where the cost of hedging is the premium charged. We saw several examples of this. If a client wanted to buy a certain stock at a future point in time, the price he had to pay for it was completely fixed. However, as we already explained in Chapter 1, the introduction of uncertainty in the form of dividends could alter the picture and lead to a discussion about the price. We showed that the cost of hedging itself became uncertain. There was still a good hedging strategy available, but the risk could not be eliminated completely. In the literature, this kind of situation is described by saying the marked is incomplete [133, 16].

The first models within the quantitative finance community were always complete, such as the binomial tree model [40] or Black–Scholes [18, 113]. Leaving room for interpretation or uncertainty in the parameters could seem like a flaw of the model. However, from the determination of the forward price, it should become clear to the reader that the world is uncertain and a lot of parameters that enter into a model are random, and it is therefore normal that each trader might have her own expectation. This leads to price competition and, if the market is transparent enough and enough players are available to provide the liquidity, the market finds a consensus or equilibrium on this.

Let us now turn to the particular case of the valuation problem of a plain vanilla call option. We wrote down the Black–Scholes pricing formula in (1.10) as if this solved the whole problem. We explained that the price was related and in fact a direct consequence of the cost of the hedging strategy, and we analysed in more detail how errors are introduced because the hedging is not done continuously. Before we move on, we would like to wipe out some more certainties the reader might have. After all, the more uncertainty there is, the more it becomes possible to challenge one's own beliefs versus the beliefs of others. If this is done on a forum such as a financial market, it is there for all to see and to join in.

What beliefs can we question and challenge? We can just go through the list of parameters in the Black–Scholes model, starting with the value of the stock $S(t_0)$. Do we really know this? Actually we don't. There is a whole series of values in the market. Typically within the market we have a ranked list as shown below.

Bid		Offer	
Value	Volume	Value	Volume
49.90	10000	50.10	15000
49.85	20000	50.20	5000
49.82	10000	50.25	10000
49.80	5000	50.30	20000

The cheapest sellers of the stock indicate that they want to receive 50.10 for the stock. Combined they make up a volume of 15000 stocks. The highest bidders are willing to pay up to 49.90 for the stock and they make up a volume of 10000 stocks. If nobody changes their mind and no new players enter the field, then the situation remains as it is with a best bid of 49.90 and a best offer of 50.10. We could say that the fair value of the stock is at $S(t_0) = 50.00$, right in the middle. Usually this value is used for pricing the option. Once we have established this option value, the trader can calculate his hedging ratio.

This means that if the trader sells N call options, he needs to buy a volume of $\Delta \cdot N$ stocks to hedge properly. That means we have to look at the offer list. Suppose the volume he needs is $\Delta \cdot N = 25000$. The first block of 15000 stocks he can buy at 50.10, however the next 5000 stocks will be 10 cents more expensive, and the last 5000 stocks he needs are again 5 cents more expensive. So he pays an average value of 50.15 for the stock. Clearly the cost of the stock depends on the volume of the delta hedge. So the question is posed whether we should have used the value $S(t_0) = 50.15$ for determining the hedge and the value of the option? In case of a call option, this would mean that the volume the trader requires is larger. If the steps between the different offers are small (with small volumes), the new hedge price could again be higher than 50.15. This vicious circle is only to be escaped in liquid markets where the volumes are much bigger than the hedging ratios the trader requires.

In theory it is even possible that the volume in options exceeds the volume in available stocks. Suppose more OTM call options are sold than available stocks. This does not immediately pose a problem if the delta hedge the trader(s) has set up is so small because the value of the Δ is small (OTM). But suppose that, for whatever reason, the market turns and starts increasing, more and more stocks will be bought by those traders to hedge their position. This again will induce higher prices, and as a result more stocks are needed for hedging. At some point the price could explode, if there is more demand for stocks to hedge with than are available in the market.

This is exactly what happened with VW on 26 October 2008, as can be observed in Figure 4.1. In the Black–Scholes model, one of the assumptions is that the delta hedging does not influence the stock price. In other words, derivatives hedgers can buy and sell without influencing the market. In this particular example, the short positions induced by short call options had to be covered. Because the option volumes were so

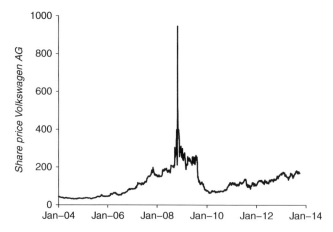

Figure 4.1   The historical share prices for Volkswagen AG from January 2004 till October 2013. One can clearly see the spike of 28 October 2008.

huge, it started moving the price upwards. Of course, this then leads to a delta that starts increasing, leading to more and volume to be covered. Since the traders were gamma short, they were running behind the market. This all blew up and made the price of the stock spike.

It is becoming clear that one of the actual risks the trader faces in the future is the shape of this bid/offer table in the future. In the Black–Scholes model we assumed that at any point in time the price was uniquely set as $S(t)$. We can take the confusion to the next level if we assume that the option has a strike of 49.85 and that at expiry the bid/offer table looks as above. The total volume for the option is 40000. If we assess that the market has a value of 50.00 at this time, any rational investor would exercise his option without question. However, if we do this and sell the 40000 stocks again in the market, we won't be receiving 50.00 because the bid levels are below this. The first 10000 stocks can be sold 5 cents above strike and the next chunk is sold at break-even value, and after that we have a loss. Similarly, one might sometimes exercise physical options if this is a cheaper alternative to obtain the stocks.

Let's look at some other values in the model. The interest rate is the next point of our attention. As we recall from the delta-hedging procedure outlined in Chapter 2, we were using a cash account, where we received or were charged an interest rate r, continuously compounded, meaning every day we would receive or pay interest. This is a nice juicy source of uncertainty. One can expect that the interest received for cash is lower than the interest to be paid for a loan. This typical bid/offer spread in the interest rate market is just the first of our problems. What's next? It is very important to realise that the interest rates are not constant [68, 22]. So we don't know in advance what the applicable interest rate is. If we have a certain amount on the cash account, we could fix the interest rate for the lifetime of the option, but only for this fixed volume. Because of the dynamic nature of the procedure, the cash on the account will constantly change and a few days later, the conditions in the market might have changed.

So, the best we can do is fix at much as we can at the start of the procedure, where we have at least an accurate view on the money in the cash account. For the future, the trader will use an estimate of the future interest rate. This should be weighted over the changes in volumes, bids and offers as executed and the lifetime of the option. Clearly there are too many unknowns in this picture and the value of the interest rate to be used in the Black–Scholes pricing formula becomes debatable once again; every trader will have his own view on what should be used.

The last uncertain parameter in the picture is the volatility σ, as this will introduce the accumulated hedging error we discussed in Chapter 2. This might be the most challenging one, as we already discussed. It has to do with future movements of the price. Combining the uncertainty on the fair value with what we explained above completes the chaos. How can you assess how much a price will change if you don't even know what the price is?

Just as the reader might think that the situation cannot get any worse, we should warn him to brace himself for more. The whole dynamics that are assumed within the Black–Scholes model itself do not match reality. The distribution of logreturns can be studied empirically and it has been done extensively in the literature [25, 35]. As it turns out, the model is flawed on the statistical distribution it uses [133]. The lognormal distribution is not quite matching and we should be using fat tailed distributions, which was already hinted in Section 2.2.

What has happened in practice over the last decades, as the trading of options has intensified a lot, is the inclusion of trading experience into the use of the model. One of the ingredients that has led to the success of the model is that there is only one parameter that is totally unobservable. The others might contain a certain amount of uncertainty, but we will explain how this is dealt with in practice.

As mentioned above, the distribution of the actual logreturns is not normal as is assumed within the Black–Scholes model. This can most easily be observed by taking a time series of logreturns and studying the statistical properties of it. In particular we know that for a normal distribution, the mean and standard deviation are the only two parameters to be determined. All higher moments are fixed. For example the skew and kurtosis, being defined as

$$\text{Skew} = \frac{1}{Var\,[X]^{3/2}} E\big[(X - E[X])^3\big]$$

$$\text{Kurtosis} = \frac{1}{Var\,[X]^2} E\big[(X - E[X])^4\big]$$

are 0 and 3 respectively for a normal distribution [105, 129].

If we use the data from Section 2.3.1 for the S&P 500 over the period 1 Jan 2008 till 1 Oct 2013, we can calculate the empirical moments of the returns and compare those to theoretical ones of the Black–Scholes model. Since the Black–Scholes model has a lognormal price distribution, the returns are normally distributed.

	Empirical	Theoretical
Mean	-0.00042	$\mu \cdot \Delta t$
Stdev	0.0291	$\sigma \cdot \sqrt{\Delta t}$
Skew	-0.3771	0
Kurtosis	14.0283	3

If we calculate the expected value over all returns, we will always find a value very close to zero. By observing daily returns, it is very hard to see the drift in a stock and the noise around it is much higher than the actual drift, as we can see in the above table. This can be explained within the Black–Scholes model by observing that in a timestep of size Δt, the drift is of order $\mathcal{O}(\Delta t)$ and the volatility is of order $\mathcal{O}(\sqrt{\Delta t})$. And for Δt small, such as 1 day, we have $\Delta t \ll \sqrt{\Delta t}$.

In any case, we already know that drift can be excluded. The second moment can be used to calculate the realised volatility. For a normal distribution these are the only two relevant parameters, as all higher odd moments are zero and the even moments are completely determined by the two first ones.

So a simple test for normality is to calculate the skew and excess kurtosis, determined by the third and fourth moment of the distribution. In the example above one can see a skew value of -0.38 and an excess kurtosis of 11 (exceeding the 3 that is present in the normal distribution). We won't set up a statistical test to verify if this is statistically significant or not, but by just looking at the values we see that the estimates are substantial enough to believe that the historical time series is indeed different from a sample coming from the normal distribution. For more analysis we refer to [59, 35, 133].

Another assumption in the Black–Scholes model is the one that states that any two periods in time are independent in terms of returns and hence also in terms of volatility (BS takes a constant volatility over the entire lifetime). In Figure 2.3, we can already visually see there is volatility clustering [145, 6, 15] which is clear from Figure 4.2 as well. We see that there are periods of high volatility and periods of low volatility. And from this clustering we see that there is something peculiar going on. This indicates the presence of a memory in the market, something that is not taken into account in the BS model.

An empirical way to investigate the realised volatility is to work with a moving window of 30 days over the time series. This time we use historical data for the S&P 500 between October 2000 and October 2013. We define a 30 (trading) day period over which we calculate the realised volatility. We then move the window by one day

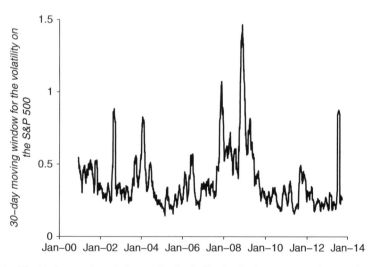

Figure 4.2   The 30-day moving window realised volatility for the S&P 500 over the period 19 October 2000 till 1 October 2013.

and recalculate. This gives us a (biased) moving estimator of the realised volatility (see Figure 4.2). We notice that the volatility never blows up completely but seems to be mean-reverting [53]. The statistics for the volatility estimation in Figure 4.2 are given below.

	min	max	mean	median	std
Volatility	14.47%	146.47%	38.75%	32.73%	19.98%

All the above observations lead us to the statement that the volatility is not just random, but also has some memory (clustering) and is mean-reverting.

4.2 Bringing Order

How can we deal with all the anxiety introduced in the previous section? The answer to most of the above raised uncertainties is trading and risk sharing. We will go through the list again and explain how this can be dealt with. After we do this, we will again forget about it and focus on bringing more insight into the model and the management and trading of options. We will then go back to the easy life, where the price, interest rate and volatility are known and the Black–Scholes model is a perfect representation of reality. As we progress through the book, we will learn to appreciate the model despite, or perhaps thanks to, its flaws. This model will turn out to be our partner. We will learn about what it can and cannot do, and we will anticipate its flaws and, as in any good relationship, this kind of team work pays off.

What value to use for the price $S(t_0)$? As a rule of thumb we will take the mid value, although it does not exist. For options on very liquid stocks or indices the volumes on the best bid and best offer are big enough to accommodate the trader for doing his hedge. The difference between the two is usually so small and the fluctuations during the day are of a bigger order of magnitude than the bid/offer spread. This means that the trader can place an offer himself at mid value, extending the table with an extra line on the offer side, making him the best offerer, rather than just taking the bid. After this happens, his offer might be lifted.

In terms of pricing, we already have some tools available for understanding the influence of the bid/offer spread on the price of the option. In fact we could argue that if we value the price and delta of the option using the mid value of the stock, whenever we want to do a transaction the market immediately jumps to the bid or offer value, depending on the direction of the transaction. The effect of this jump on the price is exactly measured by the gamma of the option. We know that the value of the option changes with $1/2 \cdot \Gamma \cdot (dS)^2$. We could substitute for dS the spread between mid and the actual market, or dS taking half the bid/offer spread. But in fact this cost of hedging does not just manifest itself at the start of the option, but will be present throughout the entire lifetime. The gamma $\Gamma(S(t), t)$ depends on the value of the stock and on the time at which we observe it (with respect to the expiry date of the option).

So the effect of this bid/offer table is path dependent. One can easily understand that if the option stays around the ATM range, where more transactions are required, the slippage effect of paying the offer and receiving the bid are more important than when the market only moves in one direction. A good trader combines his insight and experience to add a multiple of the current gamma effect to the price as a reasonable spread before rebalancing. Very interesting research [87, 146, 72, 50] has been done on this topic and the Black–Scholes model has been extended to take this effect into account in the price. For example, the Leland model [109] gives an adjusted volatility number for the valuation of long positions in calls and puts:

$$\check{\sigma} = \sigma\sqrt{1 - \sqrt{\frac{8}{\pi \Delta t}\frac{\kappa}{\sigma}}}$$

or similarly, gamma short positions should be valuated with

$$\hat{\sigma} = \sigma\sqrt{1 + \sqrt{\frac{8}{\pi \Delta t}\frac{\kappa}{\sigma}}}$$

where Δt is the timestep between hedging and κ is the percentage cost of trading in a stock.

If $\Delta t \downarrow 0$ this spread blows up. This implies that under transaction costs, you are discouraged from rebalancing too quickly, which in its extreme would lead to constantly flipping your hedge from bid to offer and bleeding the transaction cost.

Another feature that should not be forgotten is the fact that the trader typically has a big book with several options and stock positions to begin with. The marginal change a new transaction brings, or the transaction induced by the delta-hedging procedure, is much smaller than the size of the book. Typically a trader is allowed to keep a limited long or short position in the stock, so he can decide to wait a while before executing the hedging order, or to do this in parts. This is trading as at that point an open position is taken rather than eliminating the risk. This is precisely the trader's job. He needs to follow up on the risk during the day and therefore he can take positions and close them at appropriate times or, if the market turns against him, close them when the loss is getting too big.

The trader is usually not trying to eliminate risk but rather trying to manage the risk. Even worse, we showed that the uncertainties introduced earlier prevent the trader from eliminating the risks, but that does not mean that he just stands by and keeps his eyes closed.

In fact the risk management for these kinds of financial derivatives is of a completely different nature to what is used in insurance theory [67, 130, 116, 121]. Suppose we sell a car insurance with a deductible value of $K = 300$. We can write the damage risk (or cost) as X and the claim itself has the form of a call option, as the insurance company might be obligated to pay out the claim in case of an accident. The payout formula is $\max(X - K, 0)$, identical to the value of a call option. Typically the insurance company tries to determine the distribution of X, and the time horizon is typically a year, where the accident might or might not happen within that year. At the end of this year, the insurance is renewed for another year.

Although the payout of this claim resembles that of a call option, this is where the similarity ends. To see this, let us perform a thought experiment. Suppose one particular car driver buys a new car and he is exposed to a risk X. The expected value of the damage can be determined from parameters such as his age and driving experience, the type of the car and the city he lives in. Within this example we assume that the dataset of comparable risks is large enough to state meaningful numbers for the expected damage and standard deviation. Within our thought experiment, the expected damage is $E[X] = 1000$, and the standard deviation is $std[X] = 1000$ (just to keep the numbers simple). The insurance company typically buys this risk at a negative price (that is, they receive money for taking on the risk) because the risk is on the downside. This is similar to selling the call option if we want to use the language we introduced earlier.

The insurance company might put in an offer at 2000. This means they would buy the risk and receive 2000 as a premium. However, the guy with the car is perhaps limited to budget constraints or knows that he won't be using the car that much, ruling out big damages, and sees a bid value of 1000. The volume is always 1, as an insurance is very particularly written on one car risk.

Some third player might come into play and offer to insure at 1300. All of a sudden, the insurance company starts questioning its methods for setting the premium as there is a competing party. If the car owner decides to take up the new party on their offer, the risk is transferred. Now imagine that the original insurance company, afraid of losing too many customers, decides to change its policy and starts offering insurance at 1200. The intermediate player can then transfer the risk he just bought onto the original insurance company and make a sure profit of 100 because of the changed market settings. The original seller of the risk of course sold too soon, he now realises, and he could decide to try and buy back his original risk, putting in an offer himself of 1300. This last part is far fetched, but this is, of course, a thought experiment.

Let us add one more assumption into the story. Let us assume that the insurance company who is holding the risk wants to stop its activity and therefore is seeking to get rid of the risks. For risk X there is a new buyer, the original car owner. He is offering at 1300 and the risk is transferred back to him. As a result the insurance company makes a loss of -100 and the car owner managed to break even. The profit is in the hands of the speculator who joined the game.

This mental exercise might seem very artificial, and we agree with that, but in a way this is what happened in the credit industry, where credit risk [134, 45] was restructured and transferred in some way from one party to the other and trading the risk arose from that. Once the risk X is liquidly traded, we can even delta hedge contingent claims as derived instruments. At that point, the market will set the price of the risk at the equilibrium point where supply and demand meet each other. It is very clear that there cannot be a big interest in the risk X of one particular car of one particular owner. However, in the credit market these risks are pooled up into large sets of comparable risks. This is in fact exactly what an insurance book is made of, whether it be car insurances or life insurances. There exist reinsurancers [46] who are willing to take over the risk from several players in the market and in a sense this is trading, but the number of transactions is small. On top of that, regulation does not allow the trading of such risks in the same way as a bond or stock is traded and the liquidity and transparency are very different.

4.3 Internal Markets

The problem of uncertain interest rates in the context of equity derivatives is sometimes handled by the bank [80] by fixing an internal system. For the sake of making the point, we will oversimplify. Suppose you have two different desks in a trading room. The first one is the desk that trades options on stocks. The second is the desk that trades interest rates. Typically interest rates are not traded as such but through financial instruments such as bonds, swaps, and so on. Right now, we will not go into the details of the trading of interest rate instruments, but assume this desk trades the interest rate r on nominal volumes.

This will allow the interest rate risk to be transferred from one desk to the other. The management of the trading room could decide that an internal system needs to be set up to accommodate for this transfer. As we explained earlier, theoretically it is the interest rate on the cash account that we are after. However, there are so many different kinds of accounts out there. We assume the reader has a cash account himself, but he will probably know that the interest he receives is much much less than the interest he has to pay if the balance goes negative. Second, the interest rate deviates a lot from the interest rate received on longer investments.

Therefore the management could decide that the equity derivatives desk always receives an interest rate $r - \Delta r$ and pays an interest rate $r + \Delta r$. The spread Δr could be fixed internally to whatever value is reasonable. Often $\Delta r = 0$, as it is usually clear in advance if an activity will be drawing cash or is self-funding. That just leaves the determination of r. It is clear that the fixing of this is harder. However, taking the overnight interest rate [22], which would be the closest match to what we are looking for, leaves out great opportunities. A trading house typically has a good view on the value of the cash account as it has built up some history over time. Leaving the cash on this account does not make sense, and in fact the equity desk should shift this capital to other desks where it can be invested and managed more wisely [37]. Therefore one could decide that, for internal purposes, the interest rate r is taken to be the six months swap rate, irrespective of the lifetime of the option. One could even decide that the value of r is fixed once a week and kept constant throughout the week.

That means that the internal transfer is obligated and, in some cases, the interest desk is forced to take on positions with a loss, at other times it could be a profit. If the volumes coming from this equity derivatives desk are much smaller than the typical volumes they trade, this might not be as bad as it sounds. For the equity derivatives desk, it eliminates the burden of following up on the interest rate.

If the activity is organised this way, it is clear that the equity desk could arbitrage the system. If the interest rate is fixed on Monday and valid till Friday and they are looking into a transaction on Friday, and the interest rate market has changed a lot, they could decide to keep their interest rate position open and wait to deposit the cash until next Monday. An internal check-up should be installed to prevent one-sided abuse between the internal desks.

In practice the situation and the internal regulation is more subtle and each bank has its own rules, sometimes influenced by tax issues if the desks are located in different countries. The main conclusion to be drawn from this is that an equity derivatives trader should be less focused on the problem of the interest risk, and more on the value of the stock and, as we will see later, on the volatility.

In fact, there has been a debate in the quantitative finance community [92, 90, 91] whether the interest rate used in the calculations should equal the risk-free interest rate or some other number. We have elaborated in Chapter 2 how the delta hedge works and we used the concept of the bank account to justify the interest rates. In practice, desks don't have a cash account but instead they receive internal funding. This funding has become more and more the topic of discussion as the regulator has raised the question if banks have enough capital available to run their business. From the cost of hedging argument, it is clear that the cost of funding should be factored into the hedging cost and hence into the price of any derivative.

Different participants in the market will have different funding rates, depending on the capitalisation and credit rating they have. This of course leads to different internal interest rates, but also to different option prices, which they can offer to their clients.

As with all the other sensitivities, there exists a Greek that measures the sensitivity of the option price π with respect to the interest rate r. This Greek is called rho:

$$\rho = \frac{\partial \pi}{\partial r}.$$

If we ignore for a moment that we cannot trade the interest rate r directly, we could see that if ρ becomes too large for a trading book or particular derivative, the trader might want to hedge. In theory one could say we need ρ interest rates to balance the position. Of course interest rates only trade through interest rate instruments, but one can try to find an instrument that has the same ρ as the position we are after and use this instrument as a hedge in the right quantity. We will not go deeper into the interest rate sensitivity in this book.

4.4 Is It time to Look at the Time?

There is one obvious parameter left in the spectrum of options, and that is the time dimension. One would think that time is the same for everyone, albeit more precious to some than to others, but there is nothing we can do about it. When looking at the Black–Scholes formula (1.10) for the call and put prices, we see that the time enters into it as the remaining time or $\tau(t_0, T) = T - t_0$, where t_0 refers to this instant. All good and fine, let's take an example. Let us assume the volatility is $\sigma = 20\%$ and the stock pays no dividends at all (over the horizon we are interested in it). We know the interest rate r is another input, which we discussed earlier. Let's make it simple and assume someone provides us with a running account on which we can draw as much as we like or deposit as much as we like; the interest rate received or paid is always $r = 2\%$ (we should also state that we are not allowed to do anything else with our money, so we cannot arbitrage the money-market, which could be considered the price to pay to have this service activated to us).

Furthermore assume there is no bid-offer on the stock and that the current price for one stock is given by $S(t_0) = 75$. Let us try to price an ATM put option, so the strike is set to be $K = 75$. Assume today is Monday, 5 February 2012 and that the option will expire on Thursday, 10 April 2013. This means we have all the ingredients to push into the Black–Scholes formula to determine the price of a put option:

$$\pi_P = K \exp\left(-r\left(T - t_0\right)\right) \cdot N\left(-\frac{\log\left(S(t_0)/K\right) + \left(r - 0.5\sigma^2\right)\left(T - t_0\right)}{\sigma\sqrt{T - t_0}}\right)$$
$$- S(t_0)\, N\left(-\frac{\log\left(S(t_0)/K\right) + \left(r + 0.5\sigma^2\right)\left(T - t_0\right)}{\sigma\sqrt{T - t_0}}\right).$$

However, as soon as we try to do this we realise the problem we face. All entries are numerical, but the t_0 and T are now dates. Of course options expire on dates. They even have an expiration hour or predefined settlement mechanism for the underlying stock or index. Otherwise it would be quite ambiguous to know what the payout is for such an instrument. So how do we deal with time in this formula? The first observation is that the parameter that feeds the BS formula is the remaining time $T - t_0$ and not the individual time instances of calculation of the price and of expiry.

There are a lot of ways to look at this remaining time. Should we count the number of seconds, minutes, hours, days, months, quarters, seasons, years, centuries? What is the appropriate unit to use? To answer this, we should look back at the other parameters in the formula. Consistency is key here. For example, the interest rate is always an annualised percentage number, so it seems the right thing to do to use the number of years between t_0 and T. Going back to our example, it is safe to say the remaining time is more than one year. But what is one year? If we think about our birthday, or about the position of the earth around the sun, we will state that, most often, one year is comprised of 365 days and once every four years (roughly at least), we need to wait 366 days before blowing out one more candle. However, we could argue that weekends are so much fun, they don't count, making a year roughly 260 week days. One could also leave out the holidays, as they are no doubt just as much, if not more, fun than weekends, which would give approximately 250 working days (admittedly the exact number will depend on the year, the country, and so on).

Refocusing on our example, the number of days between now and expiry is 432 calendar days or 308 week days. Should we say $T - t_0 = 432/365 = 1.1836$ or $432/366 = 1.1803$ (indeed 2012 is a leap year so we had an extra day there), or should we say $T - t_0 = 308/261$ (where 261 is the number of weekdays in 2012)? The corresponding put option prices are given by 5.5766 or 5.5752. So the difference is not huge, but still substantial enough in large volumes.

Note that actually the time measure and the volatility are very closely related. While estimating the volatility, we had to make an assumption in how to annualise it (see Section 2.3.1). This question now comes back but in the reverse. So the answer to the question which day convention to use, is related to the question which volatility are you using? In any case, they should be linked together. If we had annualised the volatility with $\sqrt{365}$ we would need to reflect this correctly into the time measurement here. By looking at the BS formula, it is easy to realise that they always show up in the same combination, namely $\sigma\sqrt{T - t_0}$.

4.5   Volatility as a New Asset Class

The determination of the volatility remains cumbersome and hard. However, this is exactly why it becomes interesting, because everybody might have a different view on it. And just as in the thought experiment around the car insurance in Section 4.2, trading in this parameter can arise if there is enough interest. As it has turned out, a huge interest has emerged throughout the last decades and by now the volatility itself has become an asset class of its own. In Section 2.3.7, we mentioned the volatility index VIX. The biggest proof that volatility by itself has become a new asset class is the fact that one can now trade derivatives of the VIX index [127]. One can for example find options onto the VIX, with a strike level of $K = 20\%$ and a lifetime of $T = 2$ years. We already know and understand that options on a particular underlying asset can only be done if the underlying asset itself can be traded. And in case of the VIX index this is now possible, although it started out as an indicator.

We will come back in Chapter 7 and Chapter 8 to how to trade certain aspects of the volatility [119, 94] in a more complex setting. But of course the easiest way to trade volatility is to buy or sell an option and to delta hedge it. As we recognised earlier, if the realised volatility is below what you paid for to become long vega, you know that you will lose money while delta hedging. If the realised volatility turns out to be above the implied volatility, you will have made money after the option expires.

If we use the historical returns of the S&P 500 from 2008 till 2013, we can set up a backtest to verify the performance of the Black–Scholes model from a hedging perspective. There are various ways of doing this [73], but in our test we will take a 30 days option and delta hedge it all the way to the expiry of these 30 days. Given the fact that we have six years of history, we can have this option start on any of those historical days. Clearly we are using overlapping datasets, which creates a bias in the data, but it is a simple way to get a feel for the quality of the hedge.

Since this is a backtest or lab experiment we are using the historical volatility over those 30 days as the implied and hedging volatility. This should give us a good idea if the model performs well or not. The initial level in each of the options will be

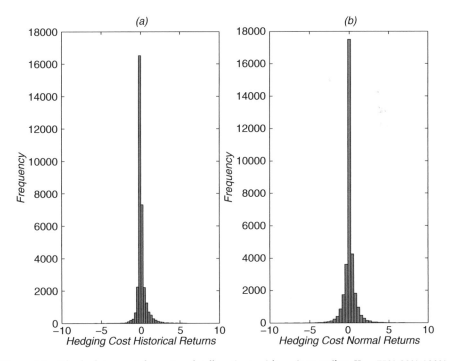

Figure 4.3   The hedging cost for put and call options with various strikes $K = 75\%, 90\%, 100\%,$ $110\%, 125\%$, each with a one month maturity. (*a*) shows the backtest using historical returns for the S&P 500 and (*b*) shows the result using normal returns.

$S(t_0) = 100$ and the 30 days of returns will be applied to this starting level for every single option. In order to make the conclusion less pointed towards the particular option we are using, we will use a universe of puts and calls with strike levels $K = 75, 90, 100, 110, 125$.

For simplicity we will assume that $r = q = 0$, so that the cash component of the hedge can be ignored. The hedging cost is then defined as

$$\pi\left(S(t_0), t_0\right) - \pi\left(S(T), T\right) + \sum_{i=0}^{N} \Delta\left(S(t_i), t_i\right) \cdot \left(S(t_{i+1}) - S(t_i)\right).$$

As we can see in Figure 4.3 the hedging cost is what we would typically expect in a daily rebalancing with the main difference. In fact the difference in Figures 4.3(a) and (b) is hardly distinguishable. The normal returns were generated to match the 30 days volatility and mean to exclude any bias between the two sample sets. The main conclusion is that the Black–Scholes model, from a hedging point of view, works well, despite the shortcomings. The difference would become more apparent if we increased the rebalancing frequency [152]. But in practice, hedging is usually combined with appropriate timing, aggregation of volume and risk taking. For plain vanilla options, the hedging is often still done by using the Black–Scholes delta.

5 Vega as a Crucial Greek

5.1 Why Vega Is Different from Other Greeks

Before we can start explaining how the trading activity around plain vanilla options came about [119], we first need to explain the effect of the volatility parameter on the price of an option. Up till now, we have always assumed this parameter to be known, at least up to certain accuracy. We already established at the end of Chapter 4 that this volatility seems to change over time. However, we were talking about the realised volatility. It might be true that there are periods of low and periods of high volatility, but once the option is sold, this will become apparent only through the hedging of the option, namely through the gamma and theta balance, which will be broken.

However, in this chapter we will just explore the effect of using different values for the volatility in the option valuation. You could say that this reflects the fact that the trader or the market changes his mind, or it can be used to take into account the uncertainty around the estimation. In the literature, the concept of unknown or uncertain volatility has been introduced for exactly this reason, which is a very useful concept but in practice too cumbersome to use.

Let us start, as we have done before, by giving the mathematical expression of the instantaneous vega

$$v_{inst} = \frac{\partial \pi}{\partial \sigma}$$

where as before π stands for the value of the financial derivative such as an option. Now why is this so different from the definition of the Δ or the θ? It just seems like any other mathematical derivative we have seen so far. Well, the first difference is actually that 'vega' is not even a Greek letter. Some readers might recognise the true but hidden identity of Zorro in this name, and just as in the popular TV show, we know by now that the volatility is the mysterious parameter within the option pricing framework. However, this Greek is so vital to option theory that we will devote an entire chapter to it. We will try to reveal the mask of vega, exposing it in all its glory.

The need to understand the vega only became important after trading options became as liquid as it is today. If you are wrong on your volatility estimate, you will only fully see the extent of this after all hedging has been completed and the option expired. Even if halfway through, you reduce your volatility significantly compared to your initial estimate, you are stuck with your position. So why do you want to know how your option changes its value if you can't do anything about it anyway? Well, if the option market becomes liquid enough [38] and everybody agrees on σ, if the value changes over time (still in agreement), you can undo your transaction. This is again what trading is all about.

Already peeking forward to this trading of the volatility, we can state that there are now three parameters in the picture, adding σ to the value of the stock S and the time (to maturity). The volatility will become a variable, so therefore we will denote the initial volatility as $\sigma(t_0) = \sigma_0$ and we write the value of the derivative $\pi = \pi(S, t, \sigma)$, which is short for $\pi(S(t), t, \sigma(t))$, and we can expand the price in a Taylor series [138] as we did before in Chapter 3 (see formula (3.3)). Moreover, we will use the short-hand notation $\pi_0 = \pi(S(t_0), t_0, \sigma(t_0))$:

$$\pi(S_0 + \Delta S, t_0 + \Delta t, \sigma_0 + \Delta \sigma) = \pi_0 + \Delta \cdot \Delta S + \frac{1}{2}\Gamma \cdot \Delta S^2 + \theta \cdot \Delta t + v_{inst} \cdot \Delta \sigma.$$

(5.1)

For all the other Greeks so far, we established expressions within the Black–Scholes model. In fact, it seems ridiculous to specify the model for the vega as the volatility and the Black–Scholes model are almost one and the same. Without the BS model there would be no σ parameter and without the σ parameter, the model is missing an essential ingredient. However, in the next chapters, it will become clear that the parameter σ can be different for every quoted option. We will see that it gets adjusted in the market, leading to the concept of the implied volatility surface. In practice this will mean that there is not one such parameter for a certain stock, but a whole matrix σ_{ij} [24] and the vega can be specified with respect to all of those. Within the scope of this chapter, we will merely investigate how individual options are driven by the volatility parameter.

The expressions for the vega for the call and the put option are given by [78]:

Vega v	
$v_{inst,C}$	$S(t_0)\exp\left(-q(T-t_0)\right)\phi(d_1)\sqrt{T-t_0}$
$v_{inst,P}$	$S(t_0)\exp\left(-q(T-t_0)\right)\phi(d_1)\sqrt{T-t_0}$

(5.2)

For most practical applications we don't use the naked vega v as defined as the mathematical derivative, but instead we normalise it. In terms of formulas, this means that

$$v = v_{inst} \cdot \Delta \sigma$$

with $\Delta \sigma = 1\%$. This is the effect of a one percentage point change (pp) in the volatility on the price of an option. Since the effect is linear, a $2pp$ change is just double this amount. There is a practical advantage to this approach. The numbers that you get in your trading book are meaningful as a $1pp$ change is a typical move that you might see. Having the vega as a number in your head immediately indicates in terms of money-terms how your portfolio will be influenced by it.

For a volatility or option trader, it is common practice to specify the bid/offer spread on such an option in terms of the vega [66]. Depending on the liquidity in the underlying, the volume of the transaction, the risk appetite and so on, he will take as a margin a multiple of the vega. For example, one can take one vega margin between the bid and the offer. So if the current level of the stock is given by $S_0 = 100$ and the lifetime is $\tau(t_0, T) = 1$, the interest rate $r = 3\%$ and the volatility is $\sigma = 20\%$, we can calculate the vega for various strikes $K = 75, 100$ and 125:

	$K = 75$	$K = 100$	$K = 125$
v_C	0.959	0.3867	0.2743
v_P	0.959	0.3867	0.2743.

We see that this approach would lead to a smaller bid/offer spread in terms of option prices depending on the moneyness of the option. Traders often communicate bid/offer spreads and market changes in vega moves.

5.2 Taking Off the Mask

Before we study the behaviour of the vega itself, it makes sense to analyse how the option price within the BS model is influenced by this parameter. Once we understand this properly, the behaviour of this new Greek will be much more transparent. Let us plot the price of an option as a function of the underlying stock level for two different volatility parameters, $\sigma_{low} = 20\%$ and $\sigma_{high} = 40\%$. The interest rate is fixed at $r = 3\%$, the strike at $K = 100$ and the lifetime at τ $(t_0, T) = 1$ year.

In Figure 5.1, we can see for both the call and the put option that the higher volatility leads to a higher price, regardless of the moneyness of the option. It is therefore said that plain vanilla options are pure volatility instruments. The higher the volatility the more they are worth.

This is all nice and dandy, but the clever reader will object right here. The other Greeks so far made sense. Delta and gamma were related to the price of the stock, theta was related to time, but vega is related to the volatility parameter. So the natural question arises. What if I know the price of an option, which is in the end something real and tangible. How do I then know the vega of this option? As we argued before,

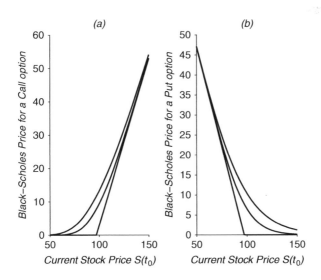

Figure 5.1   The prices of (*a*) call options and (*b*) put options with different levels of volatility.

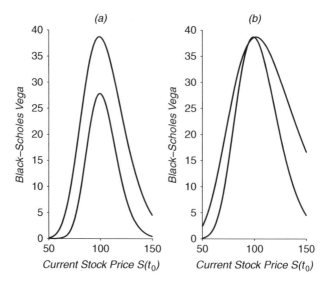

Figure 5.2   The vega profile in (*a*) is displayed for two different maturities. (*b*) Shows the vega at different volatility levels but with a fixed maturity.

one can derive the implied volatility. But this depends on the model we set out to use. In particular the concept of implied volatility is intertwined with the Black–Scholes model. So the vega is a model-related Greek. Why did people buy into this?

The reason for this is quite simple: the Black–Scholes model is so well spread that traders started using Black–Scholes lingo, and the vega is just part of this [152]. It gets a bit tricker when dealing with exotic options for which one has to turn to more advanced models. Although this is outside to scope of this book, we just want to point out that people still use the concept of vega for those as well. In particular this can be very useful when trying to hedge exotic options with plain vanilla calls and puts.

As mentioned in the previous section, a very common application in the plain vanilla market is to use the vega to quote bid-offer spreads. For illiquid markets one would take one or sometimes even two vegas as the spread between the price of the option at which a market maker would buy and the price at which he would sell. As we can clearly observe from the bell shape in Figure 5.2, the vega or volatility sensitivity becomes really small when the option is either far ITM or far OTM. These kinds of options are quite easy to hedge, at least to the extent that when the market stays in the same regime, the hedge adjustments are minor over the lifetime of the option. We saw in Figure 3.7 that the delta of a far OTM option remains small and gradually dies out to zero when the expiry date approaches. Therefore, it makes sense that the bid/offer spread for these kinds of options is lower.

5.2.1   Vega through Market Changes

It is important to realise that the vega is the highest for the ATM options, as we can see from Figure 5.2. As we stated before, options are pure volatility instruments and you get the most of this when they are ATM. Far OTM or ITM options have already picked their direction in a way. What's the probability that for a stock price of 100 a put option with strike 20 will move ITM over the next two months? We need an 80 per cent crash in the stock value before it starts breaching the strike. So whether we have an implied volatility of 20 per cent or 30 per cent, it won't make that much difference to the price of the option. Of course there is a turning point, where the impact becomes stronger again. Mathematically speaking this inflection point is defined as

$$\frac{\partial^2 v}{\partial S^2} = 0.$$

For the patient reader, it is an exercise to find an expression for this point. The lazy reader can either turn to a numerical method or use algebraic software to solve this expression to find the value σ^* of the volatility that defines the inflection point for a fixed option. For the parameters above, it turns out that $\sigma^* = 213\%$. So only if we accept volatility to be greater than 213 per cent can one expect to see a relevant contribution to its vega. In fact, mathematically speaking there are two solutions to the above equation and the second inflection point is located at $\sigma^\# = 700\%$. This is the point where adding volatility becomes marginally less important again. Obviously this range is typically outside of the normal market boundaries and should be discarded.

If we take a strike of 90, the relevant inflection point becomes $\sigma^* = 14.89\%$. So as soon as volatility is above this level, one could say the vega becomes meaningful or the option is ATM from a vega point of perspective, which indeed sounds like a reasonable level.

So flipping this around, one can ask the question how does the vega change when the market moves? From Figure 5.2 we see the curve is centred around the ATM point and decays in the tails. In fact within the Black–Scholes model, the shape of the curve is very similar to the shape of the normal density function, but within the expression of vega, there is an extra S factor that gives a twitch of bias.

Another interesting observation is to note that for higher volatility, not only is the vega higher, but the shape of the vega curve is also more flat. This of course points to the fact that in highly volatile markets the ATM point is less defined. You could say the ATM region has become bigger. This is easily explained in the extreme case of zero volatility where the ATM region collapses to a single point where $S = K$.

5.2.2 Vega through Time

The next question is how the vega changes as we pass through time. We already know that options lose their time value as we approach the expiry of the option. So it is not surprising that the volatility sensitivity or vega dies out. In particular Figure 5.3(a) shows the pattern for the vega over time.

This leads to an interesting observation. If we compare Figure 5.2 for the vega and Figure 3.8(a) for the gamma, both graphs have the same qualitative behaviour. ATM options have the largest vega and gamma compared to the ITM or OTM options. But when comparing the dynamic behaviour, it is clear that they behave in almost opposite ways. While gamma is known to spike towards maturity of the option around the strike level, it is clear that the vega dies out.

This is why if we want to capture forward volatility, we need options with the largest vega. If we want to capture spot volatility, we need options with the largest gamma. For larger vega we need ATM options with larger lifetimes and for larger gamma, we

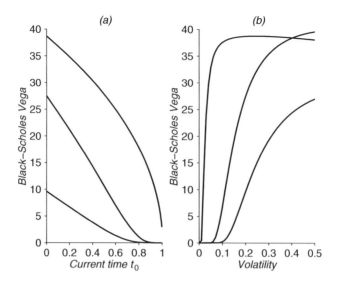

Figure 5.3 (*a*) The vega as we move through time to the expiration date (right-end point where $T = 1$) for various levels of moneyness. From the top to bottom: ATM, high strike, low strike. (*b*) The vega for ATM (top), high strike and low strike as a function of the volatility σ.

need ATM options with short expiry. We will come back to this in the next chapter when discussing portfolio trading.

It is worth noting that when the option is away from the strike levels, the vega drops very quickly with time. Only ATM options can hold their vega for a longer time. This is of course because the vega becomes less and less significant closer to maturity. Mathematically speaking there is the challenge that time passes by linearly where in all formulas there is a square root of time playing its role.

5.2.3 Vega with Volatility

The last sensitivity we want to discuss is how the vega changes with volatility. From Figure 5.2(*b*) we can see that if we increase the volatility, the vega curve becomes wider but not necessarily higher in the ATM point. This is quite interesting to realise. It means that the vega or volatility sensitivity for an ATM option does not depend strongly on the level of volatility used, at least not once a certain critical level of volatility is reached. In Figure 5.3(*b*) we look at this behaviour in a little more detail.

When we use $\sigma = 0$, of course none of the options have any time value, hence the vega becomes marginal as well. But as soon as we start increasing the volatility we see the ATM vega picking up very quickly, and it stabilises as soon as we hit $\sigma = 10\%$. After this the vega stays flat and, in fact, when becoming too large it starts decreasing again. If we use larger time to maturities, this picture remains but the stabilising effect kicks in later and the decrease happens earlier.

This might seem very strange, but don't forget that we are using a relatively naive definition of ATM, namely $S = K$. Mathematically this is not the point where the vega is the largest and if we used that as the ATM point the picture would become less blurry. But that point depends by itself on σ used in the formula, making the expressions very hard. This shows that we have to be careful with measuring and predicting behaviour over time of the Greeks, as there are many interfering parameters that make up the full story.

There are a few approximations in circulation that traders use for a quick and dirty valuation of an option price [152, 77]. The most easy is the one for ATM options. We should say, FWD ATM options as in this case the formula is most accurate, but the approximation below can still be used as a rough guideline for other definitions of the ATM point.

For (FWD) ATM call options, we have that $S(t_0) = K \exp\left((r - q)(T - t_0)\right)$, which we can plug into the BS formula for a call option (1.10):

$$\pi_C = S(t_0) \exp\left(q(T - t_0)\right)\left(N\left(\frac{1}{2}\sigma\sqrt{T - t_0}\right) - N\left(-\frac{1}{2}\sigma\sqrt{T - t_0}\right)\right)$$

$$= S(t_0) \exp\left(q(T - t_0)\right)\left(2 \cdot N\left(\frac{1}{2}\sigma\sqrt{T - t_0}\right) - 1\right)$$

so that for small $\sigma\sqrt{T - t_0}$, we can use the following approximation for the cumulative normal distribution:

$$N(\varepsilon) = N(0) + \varepsilon N'(0) + \frac{1}{2}\varepsilon^2 N''(0) + \mathcal{O}(\varepsilon^3)$$

and of course

$$N'(0) = \phi(0) = \frac{1}{\sqrt{2\pi}} \approx 0.4,$$

so we can finally derive

$$\pi_C \approx 0.4 \cdot S(t_0) \exp\left(q(T - t_0)\right) \cdot \sigma \cdot \sqrt{T - t_0}. \tag{5.3}$$

We can derive the same result for the put option or just observe from the put–call parity that for (FWD) ATM options, the premium for a put and call have to coincide:

$$\pi_C - \pi_P = S \exp\left(q(T - t_0)\right) - K \exp\left(r(T - t_0)\right)$$

$$= 0.$$

5.3 The Old Greeks Revised

Now that we have introduced a new market parameter, we need to have another look at the Greeks we introduced earlier: delta, gamma and theta. We want to understand now how they change if we switch between high and low volatility. These kinds of cross effects are crucial in understanding the behaviour of options. In fact, while trading options we have to learn how to think in at least three different dimensions: underlying prices can and will move, time will pass by and, last of all, the volatility will change over time. So far we have ignored this part of the market and we dig into this in Section 5.3.2. These three changing quantities are of course measured by S, t and σ, and the effect on the option price is denoted by Δ, θ and ν. But it is not enough to just know the direct consequences. What the trader wants to know and understand is how the delta will change when the volatility changes. This will allow the trader to anticipate the hedge adjustments and take a position accordingly.

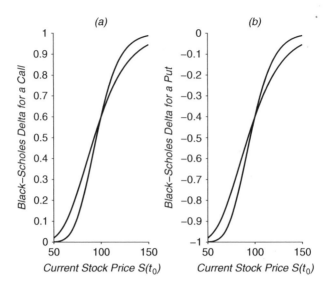

Figure 5.4   The delta Δ for a low and high value of the volatility parameter σ for call options (a) and put options (b).

5.3.1   Delta Attacked by Volatility

How can we understand the effect of an increased volatility parameter on the delta that we see in Figure 5.4? We see that the delta for OTM options actually increases and for ITM options it decreases. If we work on the premise that the market knows the right volatility that should be used for delta-hedging options, this is saying that for more volatile stocks, the delta is less pronounced. The more volatility, the less ITM this ITM option really is. Sure it is most likely to end up ITM, but that probability is lower if the market volatility is higher. Similar, the OTM option might be OTM now, but if the market is very volatile, it might just end up ITM after all.

As an easy way to remember this, one can always think of the extreme case with no volatility at all. In this case, OTM options require no hedging at all and ITM options require a full hedge (although technically speaking one could argue that even they don't need a hedge as the market is not going to move – but the sensitivity with respect to the stock price S then becomes fully set).

5.3.2   Gamma Weakened by Volatility

By observing in Figure 5.4 that the S-shape of the delta becomes less pronounced when volatility is higher, we can understand that the gamma shape also becomes less pronounced, as is seen in Figure 5.5. Again, flipping this over to no volatility, we know that the delta shape is a step function and consequently the gamma is a very sharp spike in the strike point. So for increasing volatility the bell shape of the gamma becomes wider and wider. Don't be mistaken into thinking that the gamma becomes smaller when volatility is higher. Again, the volatility impact of ATM is different from the ITM/OTM regime. In the ATM region the gamma will get lower when the volatility increases but in the ITM and OTM regions the gamma actually increases.

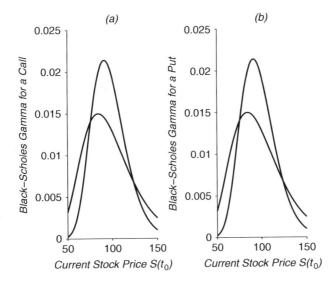

Figure 5.5 The gamma Γ for a low and high value of the volatility parameter σ for call options (*a*) and put options (*b*).

In fact the gamma and vega play a similar role to the options price. As we remember, gamma is crucial to understanding how much money the hedge is making or losing (depending on whether we were long or short the gamma). This was directly related to the way the underlying stock price would move, or in other words the realised volatility. The vega is in a way the forward measure for this. Let's start from the situation where we are long gamma through buying a put option. If the market is right and balanced, we should be paying a fair price for this and the money we can expect to make will be paid for through the option premium (and consequently bleed out through the theta of the option). However, if the market all of a sudden realises that the option was underpriced or, in other words, the expectation becomes that the stock price will be much more volatile, the implied volatility will increase, making the option more expensive in the market.

The trader then has a choice. Either he keeps on delta hedging, and indeed he will profit from this highly volatile market, or he can choose to cash in and sell the option at a higher price (in terms of volatility). It does not even matter that he might have had this option in his portfolio for some time now, as he has been delta hedging it and as such the decrease in value of the option has been offset through the hedging (remember the balance between gamma and theta?).

How much money can he expect to make over the lifetime of the option if he continues hedging himself? That amount can be shown to be identical (or at least comparable) to cashing in right now. Underlying this statement, there are of course a few assumptions, the most important one being that the implied volatility turns out to be the correct one. When you think about this, it is extremely unlikely that the implied volatility today will be equal to the realised volatility if we reach maturity and look backwards to today. Obviously nobody knows the future and even if the estimate is extremely accurate, it will never match for the full 100 per cent.

This actually gives the trader an interesting dilemma. Why? Because the market will keep changing its mind over time about the best implied volatility that has to be used. We come back to this in later chapters, but if, for now, we accept that the implied volatility changes over time [83, 24], it will provide a risk in the market. And as we discussed in Chapter 4, unknown or changing quantities call for trading. Option traders will take positions [119] when they think the implied volatility is low or high. And the money they will pick up by trading is directly related to the vega of these options.

5.3.3   Theta Strengthened by Volatility

Option prices are directly linked to the level of volatility. This means the more volatility, the higher the price. But as with anything that goes up, it can also come down. The higher the option price is, the more there is to lose in time value and quite naturally the theta gets to be smaller for most options, as we can observe in Figure 5.6. Note that smaller for negative numbers means that it gets more negative. As the vega is higher in the ATM region, we know that adding volatility to the option price means the effect is of course much larger in this region. And therefore, the theta change will be most noticeable when options are ATM.

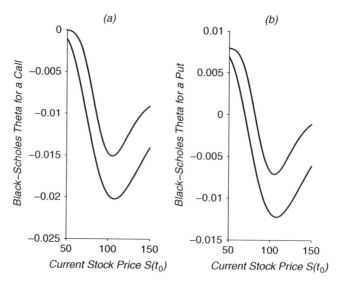

Figure 5.6   The theta θ for a low and high value of the volatility parameter σ for call options (*a*) and put options (*b*).

6 The Greek Approximation

6.1 Let's Walk Before We Run

This chapter will go in more depth into the Taylor expansion approach [103] we introduced earlier to explain some of the balances we encountered between the Greeks. Since the beginning of time, people have learned to copy from good practice, improve their observations and grow the complexity of their skillset to tackle yet more difficult problems. Some of the greatest pioneers in science have fully mastered the ability to reverse this process and to analyse complex problems and decompose them into simpler, more treatable problems that then got solved one by one. Although the hockey-stick payout of a derivative such as a call or put option is quite simple to write down or to interpret, mathematically speaking it has become non-linear, at least in the point where the option flips from being worthless to where it starts accumulating value. We already know that this transition point makes the difference between having a biased contract with only rights and no obligations, and the purchase of a stock itself.

We have also well understood by now that the value or premium of an option has an extrinsic value [152, 89]. From an intuitive point of view, it is clear that the option price should move smoothly over time, or even when the stock price moves, because if it moved very abruptly over time, it would indicate that hedging continuously does not help to manage the risk.

Now the question is, how smooth is this value of a derivative such as a European call or put option? Well, within the Black–Scholes model, the answer is as smooth as it gets [63]. This means we have a super smooth function that we are trying to understand in depth. We have introduced the Greeks in the previous chapters, and in this chapter we will revisit them, but will try to put them together into a framework. The answer to our quest was brought by Brook Taylor in 1715 [132]. Taylor realised, long before we did, the importance of stripping down complex functions into more basic functions. And it does not get more basic than polynomial functions [138].

While compiling this book, a lot of pondering went into this chapter, particularly into the decision whether to include it or not. After numerous lectures on the topic and the feedback on that, even from people who had long forgotten about Taylor and his expansion, it was decided that the benefits outweigh the risk of chasing some readers off because of the mathematics.

We will start really simply, so bear with us. 'What is the best way to approximate a straight line?' Well, this one is easy. 'By picking two points on the line and drawing a line through them.' What if there is a curvature in the line. It is quite obvious that the choice of the two points is crucial, and in fact determines the line that we choose completely. So you are saying: 'Your question has several answers, depending on what you are after. Do you want the best overall approximation of your curved line? Or the best approximation over a certain region? Or perhaps something even more local, such as the best approximation around one particular point?'

Well, now we are getting somewhere. When we are discussing hedging, we know we have a current state of the world which is set by the time your watch is indicating, the level of the stock and the level of interest rates. Since our option price is a mathematical function that has to be evaluated right now, with the current market parameters, we want to have an approximation which is accurate right now and not overall, since we have no idea what the best region to focus on in three years time will be.

Any high school graduate should be able to answer this question with his or her eyes closed, hands tied behind the back. You need to calculate the tangent line to the curve at the point of interest. For finding the direction of the tangent line, we need to be able to calculate the derivative of our value function. Now, denote the price of our derivative as $\pi(S)$ (we are omitting the time dependence as we will focus on a fixed moment in time). Then our approximation so far is telling us what the equation of our tangent line looks like:

$$\pi(S) = \pi(S_0) + \frac{\partial \pi}{\partial S}(S_0) \cdot (S - S_0). \tag{6.1}$$

Taylor expansions are basically saying the same thing as you just did, while answering my questions. We will formulate it in terms of our option price $\pi(S)$.

If you know the option price for a stock price S_0 and you would like to know the price of the option when the stock moves from S_0 to $S_0 + \Delta S$, you can use the following approximation:

$$\pi(S_0 + \Delta S) \simeq \pi(S_0) + \frac{\partial \pi}{\partial S}(S_0)(S_0 + \Delta S - S_0)$$

$$= \pi(S_0) + \frac{\partial \pi}{\partial S}(S_0) \cdot \Delta S. \tag{6.2}$$

We can clearly still recognise the equation that determines the tangent line, where Taylor is basically stating that this tangent line is a good approximation. In fact, it is the best approximation up to linear order and the error between the actual price and the approximation is of the order of $\mathcal{O}(\Delta S^2)$ [132], which is small if ΔS is small.

Now before we move forward within the Taylor formalism, we would like to point out something obvious. If you rearrange the terms in (6.2), you can easily see that

$$\frac{\pi(S_0 + \Delta S) - \pi(S_0)}{\Delta S} \simeq \frac{\partial \pi}{\partial S}(S_0).$$

If you remember how mathematical differentiation is defined [138], you can immediately see that all these concepts are very closely related and provide different ways of looking at the same thing. Before we continue, we will just rewrite the differentiated term in (6.2) by acknowledging we already encountered this quantity before in the Black–Scholes model, where we baptised it as the delta and denoted it as $\Delta(S_0)$. So our best approximation of the option price when the stock moves a little bit reads as

$$\pi(S_0 + \Delta S) \simeq \pi(S_0) + \Delta(S_0) \cdot \Delta S. \tag{6.3}$$

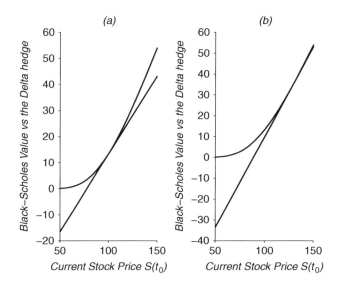

Figure 6.1   The delta hedge procedure allows you to lock in $0.5 \cdot \Gamma \cdot \Delta S^2$ when the stock price moves by ΔS. In the figure (*a*) the initial delta hedge is shown. After the stock moves up, the trader will rebalance his hedge to (*b*). The option will always outperform the hedge if gamma long or $\Gamma > 0$.

At first sight this notation might get a little bit confusing, as the first Δ is a function that refers to the delta-hedging ratio from Chapter 2 and the second delta term should be read as ΔS and is the move that the stock underwent.

6.2   Bringing Some Gamma to Taylor

If we extend the Taylor approximation (6.3) to include the next order term in the approximation, we just have to use the second order derivative of our function $\pi(S)$ with respect to the stock price. But in Chapter 3, we already introduced this quantity as the gamma: $\Gamma = \partial^2 \pi / \partial S^2$ and hence the parabolic approximation reads as

$$\pi\left(S_0 + \Delta S\right) \simeq \pi\left(S_0\right) + \Delta\left(S_0\right) \cdot \Delta S + \frac{1}{2}\Gamma\left(S_0\right) \cdot \left(\Delta S\right)^2. \tag{6.4}$$

In the previous step, we were approximating the option value by a linear position, or in other words by a position in the stock itself. We already knew that delta hedging is the best thing we can do, but now we have looked at it from a graphical or functional point of view. The approximation is better when the move ΔS is small. We can see clearly that the sign of the correction completely depends on the sign of the gamma term since the correction itself gets squared and hence is always positive.

This means that if $\Gamma\left(S_0\right) > 0$, the option price is always higher than the hedge (at least locally, because for bigger moves the higher order terms can start playing a role). We referred to this as being long gamma. From a rebalancing point of view (see Figure 6.1), it meant that every rebalancing would lock in a profit. The amount of profit is approximately given by $\frac{1}{2}\Gamma\left(S_0\right) \cdot \left(\Delta S\right)^2$ which you can just read from (6.4).

From a graphical point of view, we know that if the second derivative $\Gamma(S_0) > 0$, it means the function is convex. So you can throw out different verbal statements depending on who you talk to. You would say to the trader that you are long gamma, tell the manager the profit is positive because of the big gamma move, explain to your math teacher in high school you work with a convex function, tell the physicist you can see hedging as a perturbation. In the opposite case where gamma $\Gamma(S_0) < 0$ is negative, we recall that the position was referred to as being short gamma.

6.3 Managing through Time

We already know that there is a quantity that offsets gamma profits, this being the theta. How does this fit into the Taylor framework? We conveniently left out the time dependency in the option price because we were focusing on one given moment. But obviously the time-to-expiry of an option is an important parameter in the option price. We should include this time dependency explicitly in the derivative price $\pi(S(t), t)$ and stock $S(t)$. This makes a Taylor expansion a little bit more complicated because we have two 'directions' of change. Let's say that in a time period Δt, the stock moved by ΔS. Then our question remains: how does the option price change? Or from a trading/hedging point of view, how does our hedged position move (or in case management asks, how well has your hedge performed)?

The principles of the Taylor expansion remain the same and especially the linear term in time is simply added to (6.4). If we denote the partial differentiation term $\partial \pi / \partial t$ as θ, we can use the following expression:

$$\pi(S_0 + \Delta S, t_0 + \Delta t) \simeq \pi(S_0, t_0) + \Delta(S_0, t_0) \cdot \Delta S + \frac{\partial \pi}{\partial t}(S_0, t_0) \cdot \Delta t$$

$$+ \frac{1}{2}\Gamma(S_0, t_0) \cdot (\Delta S)^2$$

$$= \pi(S_0, t_0) + \Delta(S_0, t_0) \cdot \Delta S + \theta(S_0, t_0) \cdot \Delta t$$

$$+ \frac{1}{2}\Gamma(S_0, t_0) \cdot (\Delta S)^2.$$

In the Black–Scholes model, the time dependency is stationary, meaning that the exact time is not as important, but has to be seen with respect to the maturity T of the option. More precisely, the option price depends on $T - t$ rather than on t and T separately. Sometimes the theta term is expressed as the partial differential with respect to T and within the Black–Scholes model they differ only up to the sign. So if one uses this theta convention, there is a minus sign in the Taylor expansion (and the theta itself also switches sign) as we discussed in Section 3.3.

6.4 Beyond the Model

Traders and market participants have gotten so accustomed to the Black–Scholes and its volatility parameter, that it got a life of its own [8]. So rather than seeing this parameter σ as a model input parameter, it is considered as a market number in itself. This means it can change and fluctuate just as the stock itself does. In Chapter 8 we will come back to the boundaries of this free behaviour, but the fact that there is some freedom implies that we can act as if an option (at least a plain vanilla option) becomes a three dimensional function $\pi\,(S,t,\sigma)$. But this should not scare us off and we can just as easily write down the Taylor expansion in three dimensions as we did in the previous section for two dimensions. We will denote the current market volatility (implied volatility) as σ_0, the move in this quantity as $\Delta\sigma$ and the partial derivative by its trader's term vega $v = \partial\pi/\partial\sigma$. Our Taylor expansion reads as:

$$\pi\,(S_0 + \Delta S, t_0 + \Delta t, \sigma_0 + \Delta\sigma) \simeq \pi\,(S_0, t_0, \sigma_0) + \Delta\,(S_0, t_0, \sigma_0) \cdot \Delta S$$
$$+ \theta\,(S_0, t_0, \sigma_0) \cdot \Delta t + \frac{1}{2}\Gamma\,(S_0, t_0, \sigma_0) \cdot (\Delta S)^2$$
$$+ v\,(S_0, t_0, \sigma_0) \cdot \Delta\sigma.$$

Now there is one tricky observation that has to be made. The volatility parameter σ is very much linked to the Black–Scholes model, and as long as we price options within this consistent framework, it makes sense to investigate vega behaviour. However, if we consider two options on a stock with the characteristics $S_0 = 100, r = 2\%, q = 0\%$ and $\sigma_{hist} = 20\%$, the market will determine the price of a one-year put option with strike $K_1 = 100$ and one with strike $K_2 = 110$. As mentioned in earlier chapters, we know that the market does not follow a pure Black–Scholes model, which reflects in prices that deviate from the model price, which we will discuss in more detail in Chapter 8.

For example, for the above strikes we might have the following market prices for two call options: $\pi_1 = 8.15$ and $\pi_2 = 13.50$, which translates back into an implied volatility of $\sigma_1 = 23.11\%$ and $\sigma_2 = 21.90\%$. If we now purchase option 2, we need to clearly state that the vega is with respect to the second volatility. And although it is likely that if σ_2 goes up, the other volatility σ_1 goes up as well, their correlation is not 100 per cent. We will come back to this issue in Section 6.7.

The four Greeks Δ, Γ, θ and v are considered the main Greeks and are able to explain most of the option function's behaviour, at least in all regular cases. Why did we include the second order term in the stock move and not in the other movements? Without going into the technicalities, it is well known (at least in the Black–Scholes model) that the order of change in the stock is of the same order as $\sqrt{\Delta t}$. This in fact links the time and space movements in the model and, if we are interested in all linear terms, it makes sense (to keep the order of magnitude balanced) to include the second order derivative in the stock direction. Another way of explaining this is by saying that θ is of first order and is always balanced by the gamma as we saw in Chapter 3.

And although we started from a regular European call or put option, the expression is of course much more general than this. Taylor expansions can be applied to any well-behaved function for which the partial derivatives exist, so if it makes sense to write down this expression, it holds and the approximation is good for small moves. The quality of the approximation depends on the size of the move, but also on the higher order terms that make up the error terms.

6.5 More Greeks Than You Can Handle

There is no reason why we should stop here [60]. We have more market parameters, such as the dividends and the interest rate, and one can easily include those as well. And of course, if we are playing the game of adding more and more complexity we can go further than the line of the order of expansion. There are traders known who try to keep an eye on Greeks as high as the ninth order. We leave out the explicit dependence on the parameters and denote $\pi_0 = \pi\,(S_0, t_0, \sigma_0)$. Before we write down an expression with most of the famous and some infamous Greeks, we point out how to order them. We already mentioned that the order of magnitude for ΔS is the same as the order of $\sqrt{\Delta t}$. This means we can rank combinations as follows:

$$\mathcal{O}\,(\Delta S) < \mathcal{O}\left(\Delta S^2\right) \sim \mathcal{O}\,(\Delta t)$$
$$< \mathcal{O}\left(\Delta S^3\right) \sim \mathcal{O}\,(\Delta S \Delta t)$$
$$< \mathcal{O}\left(\Delta S^4\right) \sim \mathcal{O}\left(\Delta t^2\right) \sim \mathcal{O}\left(\Delta S^2 \Delta t\right),$$

and although we don't have an explicit link between the volatility movements $\Delta\sigma$ and ΔS or Δt. since within the Black–Scholes model the volatility is not assumed to be moving at all, we will treat $\Delta\sigma$ in the same way as we treat ΔS. The reason is that if we take an ATM option and move the volatility by $\Delta\sigma = 1\%$, the price of such an option moves by one vega, which is in the same order of magnitude as the delta impact.

First order Greeks		Second order Greeks		Third order Greeks
Delta	$\Delta = \dfrac{\partial\pi}{\partial S}$	Gamma	$\Gamma = \dfrac{\partial^2\pi}{\partial S^2}$	Colour	$\dfrac{\partial^3\pi}{\partial S^2 \partial t}$
Theta	$\theta = \dfrac{\partial\pi}{\partial t} = -\dfrac{\partial\pi}{\partial T}$	Inertia	$\dfrac{\partial^2\pi}{\partial t^2}$	Ultima	$\dfrac{\partial^3\pi}{\partial\sigma^3}$
Vega	$\nu = \dfrac{\partial\pi}{\partial\sigma}$	Charm	$\dfrac{\partial^2\pi}{\partial t \partial S} = \dfrac{\partial\Delta}{\partial t} = \dfrac{\partial\theta}{\partial S}$	Zomma	$\dfrac{\partial^3\pi}{\partial S^2 \partial\sigma}$
Rho	$\rho = \dfrac{\partial\pi}{\partial r}$	Veta	$\dfrac{\partial^2\pi}{\partial t \partial\sigma} = \dfrac{\partial\nu}{\partial t} = \dfrac{\partial\theta}{\partial\sigma}$		
Phi	$\phi = \dfrac{\partial\pi}{\partial q}$	Volga	$\dfrac{\partial^2\pi}{\partial\sigma^2}$		
		Vanna	$\dfrac{\partial^2\pi}{\partial S \partial\sigma}$		
		Vera	$\dfrac{\partial^2\pi}{\partial\sigma \partial r}$		

By using the popular names as in the table above for all the higher order partial derivatives of π with respect to the market and model parameters, we arrive at the following complex higher order Taylor expansion:

$$\pi\,(\Delta S, \Delta t, \Delta\sigma) \simeq \pi_0 + \Delta \cdot \Delta S + \frac{1}{2}\Gamma \cdot (\Delta S)^2$$
$$+ \theta \cdot \Delta t + \nu \cdot \Delta\sigma$$
$$+ \frac{1}{2}\frac{\partial^2\pi}{\partial t^2}\cdot(\Delta t)^2 + \frac{1}{2}\frac{\partial^2\pi}{\partial\sigma^2}\cdot(\Delta\sigma)^2 + \frac{\partial^2\pi}{\partial t \partial S}\cdot \Delta t \Delta S$$

$$+ \frac{\partial^2 \pi}{\partial t \partial \sigma} \cdot \Delta t \Delta \sigma + \frac{\partial^2 \pi}{\partial S \partial \sigma} \cdot \Delta S \Delta \sigma$$

$$= \pi_0 + \Delta \cdot \Delta S + \frac{1}{2} \Gamma \cdot (\Delta S)^2$$

$$+ \theta \cdot \Delta t + \nu \cdot \Delta \sigma$$

$$+ \rho \cdot dr + \phi \cdot dq$$

$$+ \frac{1}{2} \text{Inertia} \cdot (\Delta t)^2 + \frac{1}{2} \text{Volga} \cdot (\Delta \sigma)^2 + \text{Charm} \cdot \Delta t \Delta S$$

$$+ \text{Veta} \cdot \Delta t \Delta \sigma + \text{Vanna} \cdot \Delta S \Delta \sigma + \ldots$$

There is no limit to the number of Greeks one can investigate (see Haug's contribution in [151]), except perhaps one could run out of meaningful names. From a practical point of view, it becomes cumbersome to keep an eye on or form an opinion about so many risk factors, especially because their effect is typically much smaller than the classical Greeks.

Now we have expanded our Taylor expansion in all different directions and the approximation has gotten as good as we wanted it to be. How does this relate to our hedge? Will it make us hedge differently compared to the standard delta hedge? The answer depends on whether we are talking about a single option or about a portfolio of options. For a single option, there is not much else we can do. Delta hedging is the best reduction of risk and the best approximation of the option position by means of trading stocks. So knowing to a large degree of accuracy how and why the value of the option changes does not provide a way of avoiding that change occurring.

6.6 The P&L in Greek

Consider a situation with the following market parameters:

$$S_0 = 100, \sigma_0 = 20\%, q = 0, r = 2\%.$$

The premium of a call option on a lifetime of $T - t_0 = 1$ year and a strike $K = 105$ is given by $\pi_0 = 6.70$. Let's say we put $100,000$ of these options into a portfolio without any other instrument. The total value of our portfolio has become $670,477.48$ euro.

We will not add anything else to the portfolio (so no delta hedging). We move forward by one week and in the meantime the stock goes to $S_1 = S(t_1) = 107$, and the volatility changes to $\sigma_1 = 22\%$. We can use the new lifetime $T - t_1 = 1 - 1/52 = 51/52$ (or alternatively one can use seven days) and the new market parameters to calculate the premium of the same option. This leads to a book value of $1,126,797.45$ or an increase of $456,319.97$ euro. However, by analysing the Greeks we can explain this change in our portfolio value.

For this purpose, it makes sense to immediately use the Greeks at our portfolio level. This means we adjust the value of each Greek to be representable for a portfolio of $100,000$ options (this is of course simply taking the value of the Greek and multiplying it with the number of options). In the table below we can see the impact of each Greek on the one week's P&L number. In fact, as it turns out we can explain almost all of this

P&L move by just using the Greek approximation and focusing on the main Greeks only.

	Greek value		Change	Effect on the option value	
Delta	$\Delta =$	48,247.18	$\Delta S = 7.00$	$\Delta \cdot \Delta S =$	337,730.26
Gamma	$\Gamma =$	1,992.79		$\frac{1}{2}\Gamma (\Delta S)^2 =$	48,823.25
Theta	$\theta_d =$	$-1,319.56$	$\Delta t = 7$	$\theta \cdot \Delta t =$	$-9,236.97$
Vega	$\nu =$	39,855.72	$\Delta \sigma = 2\%$	$\nu \cdot \Delta \sigma =$	79,711.43
Cash		$-670,477.48$		Interest	-257.22
				Total	456,770.75

Of course, by hedging we cannot influence the changes in the option price, but we can exclude the biggest risk factor in the table in the previous example. By looking at the table, one can see that in this example approximately 75 per cent of the total P&L move can be explained by the delta risk factor. Subsequently one can state that the biggest risk driver is the underlying stock price.

Example 21 *Fortunately we can now understand that the portfolio can be hedged by selling 48,247 stocks (look at the delta and recall that this is the number of shares we have to short to balance our position). Suppose we had done this, then we know that the move upwards of 7 euro would have cost money on the hedge for the amount of 7 · 48,247 = 337,729. The reason this is not identical to the effect of the delta in the previous example is because we rounded the number of shares down to cope with the fractional numbers. The P&L of the delta hedged portfolio can be calculated by taking into account the delta hedge and will read 120,892.68 euro. This P&L can be fully explained by the other Greeks.*

It makes sense to set up a Greek table for this new portfolio containing the options and the delta hedge. Note that our cash position will change drastically because we collect a lot of cash while selling the stocks.

	Greek value		Change	Effect on the option value	
Delta	$\Delta =$	0.18	$\Delta S = 7.00$	$\Delta \cdot \Delta S =$	1.26
Gamma	$\Gamma =$	1,992.79		$\frac{1}{2}\Gamma (\Delta S)^2 =$	48,823.25
Theta	$\theta_d =$	$-1,319.56$	$\Delta t = 7$	$\theta \cdot \Delta t =$	$-9,236.97$
Vega	$\nu =$	39,855.72	$\Delta \sigma = 2\%$	$\nu \cdot \Delta \sigma =$	79,711.43
Cash		$+4,154,222.52$		Interest	$+1,593.71$
				Total	120,892.68

Now we see that the biggest risk driver is the vega term (and to a second order the gamma term).

6.7 The Vega Matrix

If we consider a collection of different options (with various strikes and maturities) and a stock position, we can calculate the Greek position of each individual option and weight those with the volumes to become a Greek position on a book level. For Δ, Γ and θ it is very obvious that they are weighted sums of the individual components. However, the vega terms actually refer to different volatility parameters, one for each different strike and maturity. And as mentioned earlier they are not completely correlated, as the market decided that options can live their own life. In the next chapters we will come back to this and show just how independently they can behave.

But if we have a volatility for each strike and maturity, the volatility view in a book is typically not represented by a single number, but by a matrix of vega terms, known as the vega matrix [24]:

$$
\begin{array}{c|ccc}
 & \tau_1 & \cdots & \tau_N \\
\hline
K_1 & v_{11} & \cdots & v_{1N} \\
\vdots & \vdots & \ddots & \vdots \\
K_M & v_{M1} & \cdots & v_{MN}.
\end{array}
$$

For a portfolio of plain vanilla options, all treated within the Black–Scholes model, it is clear that the aggregation of the vegas can be done on a strike-to-maturity basis. In practice, one might choose to rebucket the vegas into a smaller matrix by taking a subset in this matrix and assume they are a good representative basis to work from. However, those who are familiar with value at risk (VaR) concepts in a practical environment will understand that management typically prefers to have less numbers to measure risk over more. The simplest way to enlighten them is to add up all vega numbers in the vega matrix into one single vega number, as is the case in the Black–Scholes model, but this time each Black–Scholes price and Greek still has its own implied volatility input parameter.

6.8   Portfolio Effects and Exotic Structures

The complexity really reaches its peak when one investigates exotic products, because for most exotic products the Black–Scholes framework is not adequate for pricing such structures. In fact for some exotic options, adjusting the volatility (finding the implied exotic implied volatility) to match the price is not even possible because no volatility can be found such that the model produces a price that is consistent with the market price. Moreover, most exotic products are not priced with a simple model like Black–Scholes and finding the relationship between the model and market-related vega is beyond the scope of this book.

Let us go through an example that explains the concept of vega-gamma-theta hedging [152, 89]. Suppose we have a portfolio V with a certain Greek representation

$$
\begin{aligned}
\Delta_V &= 300,000 \\
\Gamma_V &= 2,500 \\
\theta_V &= -500,000 \\
v_V &= 750,000.
\end{aligned}
$$

This portfolio can come from a position in an exotic option, or even a combination of exotic options and vanilla options. Let's assume the following market parameters:

$$
\begin{aligned}
S_0 &= 1500.00 \\
r &= 2.5\% \\
q &= 0\% \\
\sigma &= 25\%.
\end{aligned}
$$

One can wonder if it is possible to design a portfolio that would offset all the Greeks simultaneously. We already know that if we want to eliminate the Δ_V in the portfolio, we can sell stocks. However, that would not make a difference to any of the other Greeks. If we want to hedge out the basic Greeks in our portfolio, we need to use instruments that have non-zero Greeks. This brings us to the option universe. Let's assume we have three options available: an OTM put, an OTM call and an ATM call option with the following characteristics:

	OTM put	ATM call	OTM call
K	1200	1500	1800
τ	1	1.5	0.5
π	27.85	207.98	25.95
Δ	−0.13	0.61	0.19
Γ	0.0006	0.0008	0.0010
θ	−0.09	−0.21	−0.22
ν	3.20	7.05	2.90.

If we construct a portfolio with the following weights:

	OTM puts	ATM calls	OTM calls	Stocks
Volume	−542,270	−1,157,791	3,673,006	227,891
Position	Short	Short	Long	Long

(6.5)

we can easily show that the Greeks for the portfolio exactly match the desired set up.

Of course the real question is how did we obtain the weights in (6.5). It is one thing to verify them, it is something else to try and obtain them. The other obvious question is whether it is always possible to find those kinds of positions such that we get back what we want.

If we define the portfolio weights as $(\omega_1, \omega_2, \omega_3, \omega_4)$ as the weights in the available options and the last weight as the weight we will put into the stock. These weights are the equivalent of the delta hedge we established earlier. We are then trying to obtain a portfolio with portfolio Greeks equal to the ones we are after. Mathematically speaking, it means we are trying to find those weights such that the following set of equations holds:

$$
\begin{cases}
\omega_1 \Delta_1 + \omega_2 \Delta_2 + \omega_3 \Delta_3 + \omega_4 = \Delta_V \\
\omega_1 \Gamma_1 + \omega_2 \Gamma_2 + \omega_3 \Gamma_3 = \Gamma_V \\
\omega_1 \theta_1 + \omega_2 \theta_2 + \omega_3 \theta_3 = \theta_V \\
\omega_1 \nu_1 + \omega_2 \nu_2 + \omega_3 \nu_3 = \nu_V.
\end{cases}
\tag{6.6}
$$

From basic linear algebra, we know that this set of equations has a solution if its determinant is different from zero, or

$$
\begin{vmatrix}
\Delta_1 & \Delta_2 & \Delta_3 & 1 \\
\Gamma_1 & \Gamma_2 & \Gamma_3 & 0 \\
\theta_1 & \theta_2 & \theta_3 & 0 \\
\nu_1 & \nu_2 & \nu_3 & 0
\end{vmatrix}
=
\begin{vmatrix}
\Gamma_1 & \Gamma_2 & \Gamma_3 \\
\theta_1 & \theta_2 & \theta_3 \\
\nu_1 & \nu_2 & \nu_3
\end{vmatrix}
\neq 0.
$$

As it turns out, if we try to use three options with identical maturities, this determinant gets to be very close to zero. The reason for this is of course that all options are similar derivatives on the same instrument and the relationship between the Greeks makes the difference between using one option or three options very small. In other words, these options are not independent enough to build up an arbitrary portfolio. A good mix of strikes and maturities solves this problem, as the set of options can be shown to form a basis in the vector space of linear functions.

In the example above we were looking for the hedging portfolio. If we put on this hedge, it is typically still a dynamic hedge in the sense that it will have to be adjusted over time and when the market moves. But because we minimised more Greeks, the resulting hedge is more stable and rebalancing won't have to happen as often. It becomes much more of a semi-static hedge [142, 86, 48, 26, 5]. If we have more options available to us, we can minimise more Greeks and make it an even better hedge.

One can prove that if we are trying to hedge an exotic derivative whose payout is only determined by the terminal value $S(T)$, then there exists a static hedge, provided we can use all the different strikes. This then becomes a truly static hedge. Of course the price of the exotic option would then be completely determined by putting on this static hedge.

In practice, one can build a portfolio with features that the trader finds desirable, for example being long vega but short gamma, because we expect the implied volatility to pick up but in the meantime the realised volatility might get violent. This portfolio exercise is the foundation for vega, gamma and theta trading. In the market one will have a whole variety of instruments at one's disposal because of the huge variety of strikes and maturities. In the next chapters we will go into detail about how these options with various strikes and maturities are related. One would think that all of them are linked through the Black–Scholes formula, but as it turns out, the implied volatility is different for all of them. This is the topic of the remainder of the book.

6.9 Long and Short the Greeks

In Section 1.8.3 we explained one can have a position in the underlying stock, long or short. Neutral or flat positions refer to the situation where there is no position at all. These concepts are extended to an option book. For example a portfolio V of a derivative π that is delta hedged is said to be neutral. As always the delta of the derivative is denoted by Δ and, when delta hedging, we will sell Δ stocks and the portfolio V will contain the derivative as well as the stocks. As in the previous section, it is convenient to add up the delta positions and this leads to $\Delta_V = 0$. Other portfolios where the overall delta exposure is a positive number are said to be long the stock and, similarly, portfolios of negative delta are said to be short. Sometimes for clarity, we will say short delta or long delta.

The positions in the other Greeks are expressed similarly. A portfolio that is short gamma is a portfolio that contains derivatives and where the total gamma is negative. More formally, one can denote a portfolio by a set of instruments $(\pi_1, \pi_2, \ldots, \pi_N; S, B)$ where B stands for a bank account or cash position. We will have a position $(\omega_1, \ldots, \omega_N, \omega_{N+1}, \omega_{N+2})$ in each of the underlying options, the stock and cash. The Greeks for each of the derivatives are denoted with a subscript. For example the vegas are denoted

$$\left(v_{\pi_i}\right)_{i=1}^{N}, v_S = 0, v_B = 0$$

and trivially the vega is zero for the stock and cash position.

Typically most Greek positions in the stock are zero, except for the delta of the stock as $\Delta_S = 1$ and the theta for the cash account. The cash account in a continuously compounding setting grows exponentially over time, and hence the theta is positive. The daily theta is given by

$$\theta_d = \exp\left(r(t + \Delta t)\right) - \exp\left(rt\right) = \exp\left(rt\right)\left(\exp\left(r\Delta t\right) - 1\right) > 0$$

with a timestep of one day $\Delta t = 1/365$. We say that a cash account is theta long and a stock is delta long. Because the delta is 100 per cent or 1, we say this is a delta one position.

Greek positions of a portfolio are calculated by evaluating the Greeks of the individual components and applying the weights. For example

$$v_V = \sum_{i=1}^{N} \omega_i \cdot v_{\pi_i}.$$

If the resulting portfolio Greek is positive, we say we are long that Greek. If it is negative, we are short the Greek or if it is zero, we are neutral that Greek. So we can be long or short the delta, gamma, vega, theta,...

Typically, to change the position in these Greeks we need to trade options. Short-dated ATM options have a larger gamma but a smaller theta. As we saw in the previous section, we can construct portfolios of any desired Greek decomposition. For example an ATM put option is short delta, long vega, long gamma and short theta. A more complex example is a portfolio of a long ATM call option ($K = 100$) and a short OTM call option ($K = 110$), both with an expiration date in one year. This construction is called a Bull Call Spread, and is long delta, long gamma, long vega and short theta. The payout of such an option strategy is always positive (see Figure 8.3), hence the premium has to be positive. With an interest rate $r = 2\%$ and dividend yield $q = 0\%$ we can price and calculate the option price and the Greeks of this portfolio:

	ATM call	OTM call	Portfolio
π	8.9294	4.9563	3.9732
Δ	57.94%	39.14%	18.79%
Γ	1.95%	1.92%	0.3%
θ	−0.013	−0.012	−0.001
v	0.392	0.385	0.007.

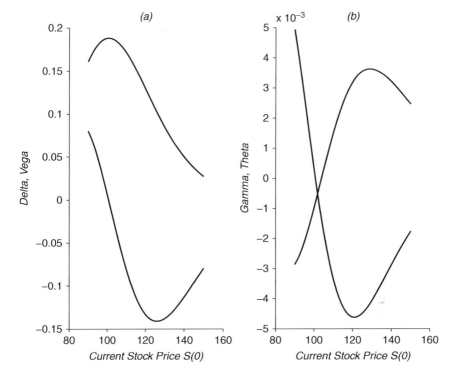

Figure 6.2   (*a*) The top graph is the delta Δ_V and the bottom one depicts the vega ν_V. (*b*) The convex shaped curve is the gamma Γ_V and the concave shape is the theta θ_V.

In Figure 6.2 we depict the profile for the portfolio Greeks as a function of the stock price. It is interesting to see that although initially the position is gamma long, vega long and theta short, when the underlying price goes up, the position switches to a gamma short, vega short and theta long position. This means that there is for example a level for the stock where the vega of the portfolio is zero. By just observing this one Greek $\nu_V = 0$, one might think that there is no volatility sensitivity. However, as soon as the stock price moves, the portfolio will become sensitive to vega again. This effect would be seen by looking at

$$\frac{\partial \nu_V}{\partial S} = \frac{\partial^2 \pi_V}{\partial \sigma \partial S}$$

or the vanna.

7 Volatility Term Structure

7.1 Why Do We All Drive a Black–Scholes Car?

So far we have talked about the Black–Scholes model and we opened the hood to display all the machinery behind that remarkable engine. We discussed the relation between the price and the cost of hedging and we highlighted all the different Greeks to explain movements of prices. So far so good. But now we want to relate this to the actual market. How convinced are traders of this model? The Black–Scholes model is wide-spread in the industry, but not necessary any more in its original form. The best comparison is the following. Say you have to travel from London to Edinburgh and you can choose any car you want. Let's make this super attractive and dream up a sunny day with blue skies, a fuel card, no time constraints to get there and nice company in the car. You caught the picture in your head? Good, tell us now which car you would choose?

Interestingly enough the answer to this question will not lead to one single answer. Perhaps people in their twenties would choose the newest make of a sports car such as a Ferrari or Lamborghini. Perhaps some people in their thirties would be attracted to a more classic make of the same brand. Elder people might prefer the comfort of a Bentley or Rolls Royce, while even others might go for an old timer such as a VW beetle. It just comes down to taste and appetite for speed, comfort, beauty or nostalgia. In financial derivatives modelling, the list of exotic models is vaste and the selection is done based on pretty much the same criteria: taste, speed, comfort, mathematical beauty or nostalgia.

All fine, but what does this have to do with the Black–Scholes model? Well, ask yourself the question: how would you travel right now? You would take the public transport or check with your partner if you can take the car for the day. Which car would that be? Well, your own car parked outside of your house. Why are you opting for these obvious choices? Well, simply because they are available, because they are reliable and, most importantly, you know their exact limitations. If you use public transport and if you have a few connections, you know you have to include a possible delay into your arrival estimate. It is not perfect, but it is workable because the solution is simple and you understand it through and through.

And would you always use the same means of transport? No, of course not. If you need to go to the shop around the corner you will walk. If you travel inside the city, you most likely will opt for public transport. Long inter-continental travels are done by plane. Usually you find combinations of different basic transport means to make it work. For example you will walk to your car, drive up to the train station, take the train to the airport, fly to a different continent and rent a car over there to travel locally.

The use of the Black–Scholes model is no different. We use it because it is available, well understood, simple, elegant and because the trading world likes it. It manages to capture the basics around derivatives' pricing quite well and in this sense it is quite adequate. Any model that tries to fix the shortcomings of the Black–Scholes model comes with more mathematical complexity and inevitably constraints as well which are usually a lot less transparent. A popular stochastic volatility model used in practice is the Heston model [81]. The calibration is usually done through use of the characteristic function [27]. However, it turned out there were two equivalent formulations for this characteristic function [3, 64], one of which had numerical instabilities [97] that made the calibration trickier.

That explains why Black–Scholes is so popular and probably always will be. Do traders believe the model? That question is answered very quickly. No. How can we be so sure that the market does not believe Black–Scholes? Well that is an easy one. It is very obvious how the market disbelieves the model and adjusts it. In this and the next chapter we will show how obvious this is.

7.2 Deterministic Changes in Volatility

7.2.1 So What's the Big Deal?

One of the assumptions in the Black–Scholes model is that the stock is stable and that its behaviour today is not fundamentally different from its behaviour in a year's time. It may be random but the level of randomness is well behaved. The mysterious parameter σ, called the volatility, is assumed to be fixed and constant [18]. However, most readers with experience or knowledge of financial markets will realise there are quiet periods in the market, but also periods that are controlled by panic and fear [145], so at best we can approximate the real world with an average volatility over the relevant period. As a matter of fact, when the Black–Scholes model gets extended to incorporate a time-dependent volatility function $\sigma(t)$, the mathematics lead to a similar conclusion as we already mentioned in (2.5).

Without going into the technicalities [152], we can mention that the averaging needs to be done in variance space rather than in volatility space. This allows for a transformation that, after replacement of the time-dependent volatility parameter $\sigma(t)$ with its average over the time period $[t_0, T]$

$$\bar{\sigma} = \sqrt{\frac{1}{T - t_0} \int_{t_0}^{T} \sigma^2(u)\, du}, \tag{7.1}$$

reduces the time-dependent Black–Scholes model to a constant volatility model. We will not prove this result but we hope the reader finds it acceptable that we look at the average variance (inside the square root) and normalise over the period of time before taking the square root again to end up at a volatility again. From an intuitive point of view, it might have been more reasonable to just take the average volatility over the life time, but the technical/mathematical problem is that within the Black–Scholes model, only the total variance is linear with the length of the time interval.

Below, we will match this with an example of hedging an option in a time-dependent volatility model which will demonstrate that the theory does work, and hopefully this will give enough comfort. However, we will refer to (7.1) as average volatility, although strictly speaking it is not, but then again, what's in a name.

Enough of maths and formulas; what is the reason to even consider a time-dependent volatility function $\sigma(t)$? Consider as a thought experiment that the lifetime of the option might be subdivided into a 'quiet' and a 'turbulent' period. In practice, this could be triggered by an announcement of the central bank or the year-end publications. However, in practice, it will never be this straightforward. For our purposes, splitting the timeline this radically into two pieces will help us understand how to deal with time-dependent volatility much better.

Suppose we have an option that will expire in 20 days and we assume a volatility of $\sigma_1 = 15\%$ over the first 10 days and a volatility of $\sigma_2 = 30\%$ over the last 10 days. Let us denote the present day as t_0, the crossover point as T_1 and the maturity of the option (and also the end of our observation period) as T_2. The instantaneous volatility function (see Figure 7.1) is just a two-step function given by

$$\sigma(t) = \begin{cases} \sigma_1 & \text{if} & t \le T_1 \\ \sigma_2 & \text{if} & T_1 < t \le T_2. \end{cases}$$

For simplicity, we will assume a actual/365 day convention and calculate the Black–Scholes duration $\tau(t_1, t_2)$ between two days t_1 and t_2 as the number of days between t_1 and t_2, divided by 365: $\tau = (t_2 - t_1 + 1)/365$. Now that we have established all the notational conventions, let's get down to business. Since the volatility over $[t_0, T_1]$ is constant, we know that the variance over this period is linearly related to the number of days in this subperiod and hence given by $\sigma_1^2 \cdot \tau(t_0, T_1)$ and similarly the variance over the second period is given by $\sigma_2^2 \cdot \tau(T_1 + 1, T_2)$.

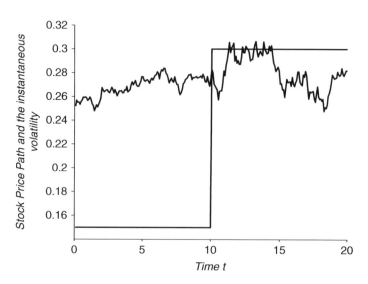

Figure 7.1 A two-phase regime with the first half of the period a low volatility of $\sigma_1 = 15\%$ and the second half a higher volatility of $\sigma_2 = 30\%$.

Within this example, we predefined that the volatility would change deterministically, so no surprise that the two periods are in fact standing on their own. The
variance over the total period is just the sum of those two terms (see Section 1.6.1 for
the corresponding property of the Brownian motion [100]). From this, one can easily
deduce an average volatility over the total lifetime of the option as being given by

$$\bar{\sigma} = \sqrt{\frac{1}{\tau(t_0, T_2)} \left(\sigma_1^2 \cdot \tau(t_0, T_1) + \sigma_2^2 \cdot \tau(T_1 + 1, T_2) \right)}. \qquad (7.2)$$

For the reader who is familiar with discretisations of integrals, it will be very obvious
that (7.2) is in fact the same as (7.1), at least for this volatility function we are using,
and with the applied day convention.

So when today, we look at an option with this particular volatility structure, we can
calculate the 'average' volatility the underlying stock price will experience over the next
20 days with formula (7.2). This gives a value of $\bar{\sigma} = 23.38\%$. Of course, tomorrow
is a new day and we can repeat the argument. The only difference will be that the first
period is just 9 days and becomes less important with respect to the second period of
10 days. In fact, we have to interpret this 'average' volatility as the average volatility
over the remaining lifetime of the option, as observed on any of the 20 days. After the
10th day, we are just in the period where volatility is at the high level, and things settle
down (note that we cannot continue to use formula (7.2) beyond that point as the first
period is over). The first term would have to disappear and the variance in the second
period is only applicable for as far as we have time left in the second period. Clearly,
the volatility is constant again, so $\bar{\sigma} = \sigma_2$. Check yourself that you can retrieve this
result from (7.1).

Adding up all those observations, we see the pattern in the table below. On the
first day, the average volatility sits somewhere between 15% and 30% as both periods
have an equal share of 10 days. Sometimes, people seem to think that the average
volatility should be the geometric average $(15\% + 30\%)/2 = 23\%$ but unfortunately
Black–Scholes life is not that simple. It is close enough though to have a rule of thumb.
Just remember the true value is always a bit higher.

Day	0	1	2	3	4	5
$\sigma(t)$	15%	15%	15%	15%	15%	15%
$\bar{\sigma}$	23.38%	23.72%	24.09%	24.49%	24.94%	25.43%

Day		6	7	8	9	10
$\sigma(t)$		15%	15%	15%	15%	15%
$\bar{\sigma}$		25.98%	26.59%	27.28%	28.06%	28.96%

Day		11	12	13	14	15
$\sigma(t)$		30%	30%	30%	30%	30%
$\bar{\sigma}$		30%	30%	30%	30%	30%

Day		16	17	18	19	20
$\sigma(t)$		30%	30%	30%	30%	30%
$\bar{\sigma}$		30%	30%	30%	30%	30%

The previous example taught us how the calculate the volatility in a simple time-dependent setting. But what should be really bugging you at this point is the question 'how does one hedge an option under such assumptions?'. There are two arguments one can make, one of which is the correct one, but we will elaborate on both as it is quite instructive. In fact Rebonato [125] proposes four different arguments, but we will stick to two.

Argument 1: For hedging, one has to use the same volatility as is used to calculate the option premium. After all, if it's good enough to find the price, it surely must capture the essentials of the hedging as well, since the Black–Scholes price formula is always the cost of hedging.

Argument 2: The above might be true, but I already know that the realised volatility is going to be a lot lower than the 23.38% I am using to price the option. So if I know this is true, then why would I put on a hedge using the wrong volatility or in other words, how can I trust my delta hedge? I would prefer hedging against movements of the lower volatility as I know these are real (expected) movements. I will adjust my volatility to 30 per cent after the initial 10 days are over.

In fact, the second argument points out another problem. If we know that the realised volatility will be only 15 per cent, we won't make as much gamma profit as we need to balance out our theta, regardless of which volatility number we plug into the delta formula. Before we come back to sort out which argument makes sense, and tackle the problem of hedging an option under time-dependent volatility, it is appropriate to clear out the confusion on the gamma-theta balance.

As a reminder, we explained in Section 3.4 that the balance between gamma and theta holds exactly through the delta-hedging procedure when the gamma profit offsets the theta loss on one day. It was argued that this corresponded to a (approximately) one sigma move of the stock, consistent with the volatility. Of course this was before we threw in the complexity of having multiple types of volatility in our conversation. We cannot argue that the stock should move more excessively than consistent with a distribution of returns with $\sigma_1 = 15\%$. That would be cheating the physical world. We have no control over how much the stock will move. In particular, the one standard deviation move of the stock return over one day (ignoring the drift term as this is negligible over one day compared to the volatility impact), is given by $\ln S(t_0 + 1)/S(t_0) = \sigma_1 \sqrt{1/365}$ (see Section 2.3.1). This leads to a simple relationship of

$$S(t_0 + 1) = S(t_0) \cdot \exp\left(\sigma_1 \sqrt{1/365}\right), \tag{7.3}$$

so if our starting value is $S(t_0) = 100$, the next day's one sigma move is $\Delta S = S(t_0 + 1) - S(t_0) = 100.79 - 100 = 0.79$.

7.2.2 Theta Looks at Vega

Going back to the same example where the volatility of the stock over the lifetime of the option (20 days) follows the two-step function in (7.2), we will now analyse the quality of a hedge overnight. Assume the strike level is $K = 99$ and the current stock price is at $S(t_0) = 100$. For simplicity we will assume $r = q = 0\%$ (for those of you who are worried about this assumption, we are coming back to this in the next section). Using the average volatility to price the option of $\bar{\sigma}(t_0) = 23.38\%$, we see that the price of a put option is given by $\pi(t_0) = 1.76$.

When moving to the next day $t_0 + 1$, there are two effects that take place on the valuation of the same option, now with an expiry in 19 days. First, there is the usual loss of theta. We know how much this is by plugging all the parameters into (3.6) : $\theta = -0.05$. The value for gamma is $\Gamma = 0.07$, so this means that the gamma profit (remember it is quadratic?) is $1/2 \cdot \Gamma \cdot \Delta S^2$ where $\Delta S = S(t_0 + 1) - S(t_0) = 0.79$ in our example. This gives a cash gamma (3.5) profit of $\Gamma_{P\&L} = 0.02$, which is clearly not enough to compensate the theta loss of 5 cents.

The followers of Argument 2 should be on their feet now, saying that I just proved their point. That it all has to do with the number of stocks we hedged with. But please, sit down again and stay quiet until the next section. We will come to that soon enough. There is one other important point to make first.

When we have moved to the second day, the pricing volatility is no longer $\bar{\sigma}(t_0) = 23.38\%$, as we can cross off one day from the low-volatility calendar. From the previous table, we see that the new pricing volatility is in fact higher and given by $\bar{\sigma}(t_0 + 1) = 23.72\%$. So the same option is priced with a higher volatility on the next day. Wait, that's great, so the option becomes relatively more expensive by itself. And we know how much more expensive as we know the vega concept. For this particular option, on day t_0, the vega is given by $v = 0.09$. So the vega effect of $v \cdot (23.72 - 23.38) = 0.03$.

Adding all effects up gives a gamma profit of 3 cents, a (predictable) vega profit of 2 cents and a (predictable) theta loss of 5 cents. There you go, we have re-established the gamma-theta balance, but we need to include the vega component to make the numbers stick.

We can actually formalise the above by going back to the Taylor [7] expansion (5.1) :

$$\pi(S_0 + \Delta S, t_0 + \Delta t, \sigma_0 + \Delta\sigma) = \pi_0 + \Delta \cdot \Delta S + \frac{1}{2}\Gamma(\Delta S)^2 + \theta \cdot \Delta t + v \cdot \Delta v.$$

In the case of our time-dependent volatility model, we can say that the average volatility function becomes time-dependent as well (as its value depends on the day we are using it), $\bar{\sigma} = \bar{\sigma}(t)$, and we know $\Delta\sigma$ over one day is related to the change in time. In fact, by using (7.1) and some simple algebraic approximations such as

$$\frac{b}{a + \varepsilon} = \frac{b}{a} - \frac{b}{a^2}\varepsilon \text{ for } \varepsilon \text{ small} \tag{7.4}$$

$$\sqrt{a + b\delta} = \sqrt{a} + \frac{1}{2}\frac{b}{\sqrt{a}}\delta \text{ for } \delta \text{ small} \tag{7.5}$$

one can find an approximation for the change in volatility overnight:

$$
\Delta\sigma = \sqrt{\frac{1}{T-(t_0+\Delta t)} \int_{t_0+\Delta t}^{T} \sigma^2(t)\,dt} - \sqrt{\frac{1}{T-t_0} \int_{t_0}^{T} \sigma^2(t)\,dt}
$$

$$
= \frac{1}{2} \frac{\bar{\sigma}^2(t_0) - \sigma^2(t_0)}{\bar{\sigma}(t_0)} \frac{\Delta t}{T-t_0} \tag{7.6}
$$

$$
= \hat{\theta} \cdot \Delta t
$$

with

$$
\hat{\theta} = \frac{1}{2} \frac{\bar{\sigma}^2(t_0) - \sigma^2(t_0)}{\bar{\sigma}(t_0)(T-t_0)}.
$$

So this means that we can in fact rearrange the terms in the Taylor expansion above and include the vega term in the theta term, and get an effective theta which is a combination of the regular Black–Scholes theta and the vega term addition:

$$
\theta_{\text{eff}} = \theta + v \cdot \hat{\theta}.
$$

This tackles the first problem. While holding the option, one does not have to make back the pure theta θ, but the effective theta, and in our case the second term is of a different sign to the regular theta because the average volatility $\bar{\sigma}(t_0)$ increases over time and this increases the value of the option over time.

EXERCISE 23

Unless you have encountered the approximation formulas (7.4) and (7.5) before and believe them straight away, verify them by using a Taylor expansion around $x = 0$ on $f_1(x) = \frac{b}{a-x}$ and $f_2(x) = \sqrt{a+bx}$.

EXERCISE 24

If you like algebraic equations, please verify this one (7.6).

7.2.3 Hedging Under Term Structure

Now we are ready to return to the original question: should we hedge against the instantaneous volatility $\sigma(t_0)$ or against the average future volatility $\bar{\sigma}(t_0)$? Let's make the two-step volatility process even more simple. If we assume that during the first 15 days the stock price will not move at all, or in other words if we set $\sigma_1 = 0$, we can ask the question again: should we put on a hedge at all during those 10 days?

In our previous numerical examples we had $r = q = 0$, so for the moment we will stick with this. This means that borrowing money does not cost us anything as there is no interest due on the amount, nor do we receive any interest for capital. We will lift that assumption below, but for now it just eliminates some unnecessary complexity. We are still using the same OTM put option as in the previous section. The two values of volatility we are considering to use are $\sigma_1 = 0$ and $\bar{\sigma} = 20.70\%$. The corresponding delta values are $\Delta(\sigma_1) = 0$ (since it is an OTM option there is no hedge required) and $\Delta(\bar{\sigma}) = -0.41$.

So the followers of Argument 1 are saying that for every 100 put options long, we have to buy 41 stocks today, although we already know that the stock price won't move for the next 10 days. The followers of Argument 2 are saying that we should not put on a hedge until the 10th day when volatility will kick in. Well, the witty reader could argue: does it even matter? Whether we put on the hedge now or in 10 days, stock price is going to be the same and there is no interest rate playing a role. True, but what about the value of the option? Isn't this going to change from one day to the next? Shouldn't we look at the effective theta? Well, yes and no. It is true that the value of an option will decay over those 10 days (theta-effect), but it is also true that the volatility will increase over those 10 days. And the beauty of the whole framework is that in case $\sigma_1 = 0$, those two effects are equal and cancel each other out, so the option value does not change over the first 10 days if the instantaneous volatility is zero, although the average forward looking volatility is changing every day. In fact, even our regular theta changes from -5 cents on the first day to -9 cents on the 10th day as can be observed from the table below.

Day	$\bar{\sigma}$	Put option	$\Delta(\bar{\sigma})$	θ	ν	θ_{eff}
0	20.70%	1.51	−0.41	−0.05	0.09	0.00
1	21.21%	1.51	−0.41	−0.05	0.09	0.00
2	21.76%	1.51	−0.41	−0.05	0.09	0.00
3	22.36%	1.51	−0.41	−0.05	0.09	0.00
4	23.01%	1.51	−0.41	−0.06	0.08	0.00
5	23.72%	1.51	−0.41	−0.06	0.08	0.00
6	24.49%	1.51	−0.41	−0.07	0.08	0.00
7	25.35%	1.51	−0.41	−0.07	0.08	0.00
8	26.31%	1.51	−0.41	−0.08	0.07	0.00
9	27.39%	1.51	−0.41	−0.08	0.07	0.00
10	28.60%	1.51	−0.41	−0.09	0.07	0.00

Before we extend, we would like to make an observation here that hopefully makes the reader appreciate the beauty that comes with the Black–Scholes model and formula. We know that the value of Δ is a non-trivial function of time and volatility:

$$\Delta_C = N\left(\frac{\log\left(S(t_0)/K\right) + \frac{1}{2}\bar{\sigma}^2(t_0) \cdot (T - t_0)}{\bar{\sigma}(t_0) \cdot \sqrt{T - t_0}}\right),$$

and it appears from the table above that the delta remains constant while time changes and consequently $\bar{\sigma}$ changes. You have to admit, it is nice when intuition and math come together.

Now what happens if we throw in interest rates? What should we do? Regardless of anything else, our first instinct should be to want to sell the stock. If we sell the stock, collect the cash, put it in the bank, collect the interest and buy back the stock for the same price on day 10, it will be happy days. Wait, where did this go wrong? Where did we introduce an arbitrage into the story? Well, we just proved that if something is guaranteed to hold its value, and is liquid enough to trade in and out of, you should sell it now and play bank. Looking back at (7.3), we ignored the drift term. In Section

1.3 we explained how the forward value of a stock should be calculated and in fact zero volatility will mean that the forward value of the stock won't change, rather than the stock price. This would eliminate the arbitrage again and take away our happy days.

Since the value of the delta only depends on the price of the stock through the forward price (see (1.10)), we will still have a constant Δ over the first 10 days. And although the values for the other Greeks are altered, the effective theta remains zero. And since we just argued that selling stock is in balance with a constant forward price, we can safely say that in case $\sigma_1 = 0$, the followers of both Argument 1 and Argument 2 were right.

But is it always true that it does not matter? Of course not. We were focusing on the example where the stock was in fact deterministic and its value was completely predictable. If we throw in randomness, things change, but the insights we have built up in this chapter still hold. Let us go back to the original example where $\sigma_1 = 15\%$. The table below contains all parameters and resulting Greeks on the first day $t_0 = 0$. The interest rate and dividend yield $r = q = 0$ again, as this allows the reader to reconcile the numbers from before more easily.

Day	$\sigma(t_0)$	$\bar{\sigma}(t_0)$	Put option	$\Delta(\sigma)$	$\Delta(\bar{\sigma})$	Γ	ν	θ	θ_{eff}
0	15%	23.38%	1.76	−0.38	−0.42	0.07	0.09	−0.05	−0.02
1	15%	23.72%	1.43	−0.30	−0.36	0.07	0.09	−0.05	−0.02

Why don't we make a distinction for the other Greeks between which value of σ we plug in? The reason is simply because the other Greeks help us explain the change in option price through the Taylor expansion. It is only the delta that tells us to go out to the market, and it determines the size of our hedge. We can simply put both arguments next to one another and compare to see which is the better hedge if the stock moves one standard deviation (of course one standard deviation that is consistent with $\sigma_1 = 15\%$) or from $S(t_0) = 100$ to $S(t_0 + 1) = 100.79$ making $\Delta S = 0.79$.

To get rid of the decimal numbers, we assume we hold 100 put options rather than just one. Under the instantaneous volatility, we should buy 38 stocks at a price of 100 per stock to offset our position. The negative cash flow is $-38 \cdot 100 = -3800$. On the next day, the stock price has gone up by 0.79 per stock, and when we close out the position we see a profit of $38 \cdot 0.79 = 30$. But what about the value of our puts? Each put has gone down by 33 cents, so on the 100 put options, this leads to a loss of $0.33 \cdot 100 = 33$, giving the portfolio an overall loss of 3 or 0.03 per put. Hence, although we are long gamma and the stock moved by one standard deviation, we see a loss in our portfolio. This means that we did not hold enough stocks to compensate for the put options.

What about Argument 1: does this work better? In that case we would have bought more stocks so that is promising. The number of stocks for the same portfolio that Argument 1 prescribed is 42 stocks, so the profit after the same move would have been $42 \cdot 0.79 = 33$, matching the actual loss on the put options.

Is this just a coincidence? No, of course not, and in fact we could have seen this from the comparison of the theta and the effective theta. Since the effective theta is lower, we know that we don't really need to compensate for the lower volatility. We can stick with the same weapons, and our break-even point is already adjusted through the effective theta.

7.3   Market Term Structure

Now that we understand the basics of volatility term structure, we are ready to ask the question how term structure behaves in the market? The market indeed acknowledges that there are periods of low volatility and periods of high volatility. In fact, the volatility tends to cluster over time. For example, there might be a period of crisis, poor liquidity or a bad economic outlook in which the volatility of the stock market is high. Gradually, as the situation improves, the financial markets will settle down and turn from a volatile period into a more stable state. Most often, it takes a bit of time for the market to settle down and volatility decreases gradually to lower levels.

The typical volatility term structure for ATM options is an increasing function to reflect the risk factor in the stochasticity of the volatility. A typical ATM term structure is shown in Figure 7.2. We can see that the very near-expiry options carry a larger risk premium, which is due to the jump risk.

In Section 7.2 we started from a time-dependent volatility function to calculate the average volatility and hence the option prices. Can we do the reverse as well? Given the term structure $\sigma_{imp}(t_0, T)$, can we derive the instantaneous volatility function $\sigma(t)$? The answer is yes and it can be shown [56, 57, 152] that the formula is given by

$$\sigma(t) = \sqrt{\sigma_{imp}^2(t_0, t) + 2(t - t_0)\sigma_{imp}(t_0, t)\frac{\partial \sigma_{imp}(t_0, t)}{\partial t}}. \qquad (7.7)$$

From this formula, we can see that there have to be restrictions on which term structures are valid ones. If the expression in the square root becomes negative, then

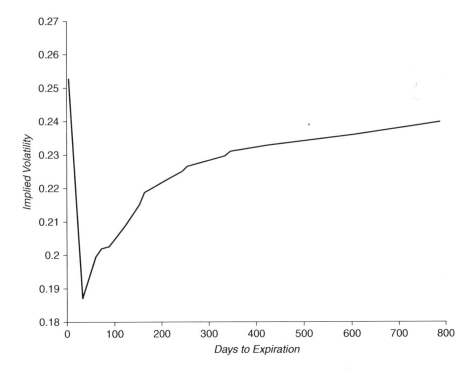

Figure 7.2   The ATM volatility term structure of the S&P 500 on 19 October 2009.

the square root becomes a complex number. So we can understand that one cannot just plot any function $\sigma_{imp}(t_0, T)$ and expect this to be without arbitrage. This problem typically arises when the term structure is decreasing with maturity. In this case the partial derivative $\partial \sigma_{imp}(t_0, t)/\partial t < 0$. We will use an discrete example to illustrate this.

Example 25 *Assume we have two maturities given $T_{1,2} = 1, 2$ and the corresponding volatilities are $\sigma_1 = 20\%$ and $\sigma_2 = 10\%$. As in Section 7.2.1, we turn to the variance. The variance over the first year is given by $\sigma_1^2 (T_1 - t_0) = 0.04$. The variance over the two years combined is given by $\sigma_2^2 (T_2 - t_0) = 0.02$. This means that the variance in the second year has to be negative, which gives a contradiction.*

It is one thing to say we shouldn't have volatilities that lead to such a negative variance, but what if the market trades these? What would this mean? One can expect that this leads to an arbitrage. We will now show how to take advantage of this by retaking Example 25.

Example 26 *Take an initial stock price of $S_0 = 250$ and for simplicity assume $r = q = 0\%$. Let's consider the following strategy. Sell a one-year ATM call option with volatility $\sigma_1 = 10\%$, priced 19.91 euro and buy a two year ATM call option with volatility $\sigma_2 = 20\%$, priced 14.08 euro. By using the prices, one can immediately see we are collecting money to put this strategy in place. However, at the expiry of the first option, we know that the second option will have a value above the intrinsic level, hence no matter what the payout is for the short position we can then sell the second option (which still has a lifetime of one year) and collect extra premium above the intrinsic value. This leads to an arbitrage.*

Now that we clarified the arbitrage opportunity, it has become clear that the relationship that we are using to rule out the arbitrage is

$$T_1 \leq T_2 \implies \pi_C(t_0, K, T_1) \leq \pi_C(t_0, K, T_2) \tag{7.8}$$

or that calendar spreads are positive. This is also known as the convex order.

One can show that this is one of the sufficient conditions to be arbitrage free as well [28, 41, 110]. We will state the other condition in the next chapter.

8 Skew and Smile

8.1 What Can We Really Imply?

As we explained in Section 2.3.5, the implied volatility is basically set by two things: the market price of an option and the Black–Scholes formula. It is quite important to realise that this implied volatility is entangled with the Black–Scholes model. It is the mysterious parameter σ in the Black–Scholes model such that the model price equals the market price. If the model were to be perfect, we could follow the following recipe: pick one option arbitrarily, for example an ATM option with an expiry of approximately one year (or whichever maturity is closer to the one year one). We can then go into the market and find out how much we have to pay for this option. As the only reality is the cashflow associated with this purchase, we use this cash price to then determine what the implied volatility is in the Black–Scholes model such that the model price and market price match exactly. Once we found the volatility, if the model is perfect, we are pretty much set. After all, the σ parameter determines how much the underlying price will move up and down, at least statistically speaking. Theoretically, we should be able to price any other option, even if the strike is different. Admittedly, as we saw before in Chapter 7, one can understand that implied volatility can and in fact should depend on the hedging period, but at least for identical maturities one would expect this argument to hold.

This all used to be true. However things changed quite dramatically after the big financial crisis in the 1990s [31]. As a result of this event, the market changed and options with identical maturity but different strikes started being priced off a different volatility parameter. This might seem very strange, considering that the hedging of each instrument will of course be done with the same underlying stock or index. Why does the ATM option imply a different volatility for the underlying price than the ITM option? That is the million dollar question [8]. Some people go as far as to try and predict market moves by investigating the patterns observable in the implied volatility, which we will touch upon in Section 8.5.3.

8.2 How Do We Start Smiling?

If we observe all the options with a single fixed maturity and calculate for each one of those the implied volatility, and plot these as a function of the strike on a graph, one can observe a variety of different shapes and forms, depending on the specific market, market conditions, the maturity involved, market participants, and so on. This pattern is called the smile or skew and can be observed in Figure 8.1.

The best way to understand how the 'skew' comes about is to put ourselves in the shoes of a derivatives trader who has a bunch of clients coming to him to buy options, all with a one-year expiry (for simplicity). We will assume all the analysis is done and we can come up with the 'right' forecast of the volatility σ for the underlying price for the next year. Some of those clients are asking for ATM options, but the biggest proportion of the clients are looking for protection on the downside, so they are looking to purchase OTM put options. Finally, the last group is looking for profit taking and they are looking to sell OTM call options.

Let's turn to an example to make it even more specific. The underlying index price is $S_0 = 1500$ euro, the market interest rate over one year is $r = 2.5\%$, the dividend yield is $q = 1.2\%$ and the volatility the trader came up with as the right one is given by $\sigma = 18\%$. Assume there are 100 clients in total, out of which 20 want to buy the ATM call option, 30 want a 10% OTM call option, 25 want a 10 per cent OTM put and another 25 want a 20 per cent OTM put. As a first step, the trader prices all the relevant options with the relevant volatility.

	20 put	10 put	ATM call	10 call
Strike	1200	1350	1500	1650
Model price	10.49	38.49	115.45	58.62
Margin-adjusted price	12.00	40.00	116.50	60.00
Margin implied volatility	18.66%	18.33%	18.18%	18.25%

As is obvious from the second line in the table above, the OTM prices are quite low in notional amounts compared to the ATM option. Supply and demand will naturally make the trader try and take a margin. If there is a lot of competition amongst the sellers, the margin adjustment will be smaller. Obviously there might be a discrepancy in opinion between various traders on that level of the volatility, but for the sake of argument and simplicity we will assume that everyone agrees on this.

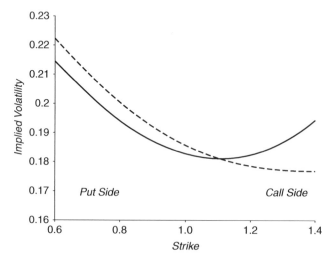

Figure 8.1   A typical smile (skewed) shape in the full line and a skew shape in the dashed line for the implied volatility. The put-side corresponds to the low strikes and the call-side to the high strikes.

The OTM options are typically bought as an insurance. For example, pensions funds sometimes have rolling schemes where they buy put options for a certain notional volume related to the assets under management. Once these options expire, they will roll into new put positions. This is done to protect the investors against the downside risk in equity markets. It is very tempting to add a bit of margin to all these prices. Let's assume the trader adds a similar premium to the option price to bring it up by approximately 1.50 euro and then rounds the number as in the table above.

Out of those new prices, we can then calculate back what the implied volatility for these options is. As one can read off in the table above, the effect of this fixed premium is of course much larger on the OTM options because the vega is much smaller. Smile is born. This exercise shows that margin adding leads to what is known as smile behaviour, not because margin makes the trader smiles (although that is true as well), but because a plot of these new implied volatilities versus the strike gives a smiling face (see the full line in Figure 8.1).

The spectrum of low strikes is referred to as the put-side and the range of high strikes as the call-side. As in the example above, one often only looks at OTM options. Of course the put–call parity relates the prices of OTM calls to ITM puts. However, typically ITM products are less interesting as they have a large intrinsic value embedded in them and as such they are cash-intensive to trade.

8.3   How Does a Smile Turn into a Smirk?

We will build further on the previous example. We know from the previous chapters that the trader will manage this portfolio of options by delta hedging each of those short positions. We also learned that this will go well for as long as the realised volatility does not exceed the volatility he sold at. So looking across the various volatilities in the table in the previous section, as long as the realised volatility does not exceed 18.66 per cent, things will go well for the trader and he will not lose any money while delta hedging his positions.

We also know that on days where the realised volatility is high, the trader will lose money as he is short gamma on each of those options. What else do we know? It is very important to realise that on these days, the option that is closest to ATM will cause the biggest grief as this one has the highest gamma. Furthermore, if the maturity is closer, the pain will be bigger.

Now imagine the following scenario. A few days after the trader sold all those options, there is a big market crash. This means indices and stock prices drop 10–20 per cent over the span of a few days. What is very typical after such a large correction is that the market gets very nervous, which is reflected by larger daily and intraday volatility. This increased volatility is often long-lived and only dies out very slowly over time as and when markets stabilise again.

In this scenario, there are a few observations to be made. The trader will overall lose money while hedging because of his short gamma position and the high realised volatility. But if we analyse in a bit more detail which options will be the main cause of this loss, it is not the call options that were originally ATM, nor the OTM call options. After the crash, both of those have become OTM options with a very small gamma and vega and therefore relatively harmless. Note that even on those positions, the trader will continue to lose money, but only in very small quantities. The most harm is coming from the puts that were originally OTM and have now become ATM, which means the gamma went up.

The trader sold insurance to his clients, but he got bitten by the downside risk himself and, of course, once bitten, twice shy. OTM puts will get a higher risk premium over the ATM options. One can start wondering if the same risk holds on the higher strike where he sold the OTM call options. A typical pattern in equity markets is that when markets calm down, markets start rallying. So it is therefore normal to actually expect a lower volatility regime once the OTM calls become ATM. Because of this, the implied volatility trades at a discount versus the ATM level. Figure 8.1 (dashed) shows such a pattern, which is now known as skew, and even to date this is the persistent pattern in the equity markets. To be very precise, it is in fact a negative skew, but usually people refer to it as just skew.

How about other markets such as FX, commodities, interest rates, and so on? Would we see skew there as well? Every market has its own behaviour participants and risk profile. Therefore the volatility patterns are also particular for each asset class. For example, foreign exchange markets [33] are less prone to the above described behaviour as they tend to be more symmetric. After all, a drop in USD versus EUR or a drop in EUR versus USD might have identical impacts but on other sides of the Atlantic. Commodities [65, 34] often exhibit an inverse or positive skew because the risk sits on the upside. If commodities prices rise very sharply, this becomes a risk for industrials who process these commodities into their final products. They are often looking for protection on the upside, flipping the story around. Interest rates [22] have their own behaviour depending on what instrument is being considered.

8.4   Skew Is Not a Crystal Ball

People started turning to the volatility skew as a new point of view in the market. If there is a very strong negative skew, the market surely anticipates a crash, one could say. This is a very interesting statement and it could be true, but it has to be seen in the proper context. If a lot of people expect a crash, they might try to buy protection via OTM put options. At the same time, nobody will be interested in selling this protection if the consensus is that there will be a crash. Prices for these OTM put options will rise and as a consequence the implied volatility as well, and hence the skew sharpens.

Can we say the converse as well? If we see this pattern, it must mean the market is expecting a crash? Obviously not. The only thing we know for sure is that there is more demand than supply (and hence prices go up). There can of course be different reasons why this happens. Using the implied volatility to predict the direction of the market is very difficult, perhaps even impossible [8]. It brings us back to the very basics of the Black–Scholes model. The price is set by the anticipated cost of hedging. If anything, this cost is related to the magnitude of moves or volatility rather than the direction of the market.

There is another reason why one has to be careful with too much interpretation. It is a well-known fact that over time the returns of equity prices behave much more erratically than is described by the Black–Scholes model. In practice, this means that larger moves occur more often than the Black–Scholes model would allow and being gamma short is of course a dangerous position to be in. Historical analysis shows that downside risk is also more pertinent than upside risk and hence the negative skew in equity markets (see Section 4.1 for a numerical example of the empirical skew) is in fact the default to be expected. Of course the magnitude of the skew can be different at different times.

How would we set the 'appropriate' level of skew? Let's keep working with the above example. We will of course have to rely on a few assumptions to come to a final answer, but this is what financial modelling is about. You try to quantify assumptions and calculate or analyse what they imply. Our starting point was that $\sigma = 18\%$, but we need to ensure that there is enough buffer built in for a crash. We will make some simple arguments here, because of course, in the end, it is the market that sets the price balancing supply and demand of the interest in options.

Let's focus on the 10% OTM put option that needs pricing. The price calculated by the Black–Scholes formula for $\sigma = 18\%$ reads 38.49 euro. We also know that the gamma of this option is given by $\Gamma = 0.0011$. As we explained in Chapter 3, this means that if the index crashes by 10 per cent, we have a negative P&L impact in our book of

$$\frac{1}{2}\Gamma \cdot (\Delta S)^2 = 0.5 \cdot 0.0011 \cdot (1500 - 1350)^2 = 12.375.$$

When we use the word 'crash' we assume this move happens in one day, so the related theta profit (if we sell the option, we are long theta) is given by $\theta_{1d} = -0.0956$. This means that the balancing move or normal move would be the move ΔS that would offset both the gamma loss and the theta profit, or:

$$\frac{1}{2}\Gamma (\Delta S)^2 = 0.0956,$$

and from this we can calculate that a 'normal' one day move would have been $\Delta S = 13.16$ euro instead of the 150 euro crash. If this is the only special move we want to protect ourselves against, we can charge the gamma loss, corrected for the theta profit as a risk premium to the option price. This brings our option price from 38.49 to 50.77 euro. From this we can back out the implied volatility again and find that $\sigma_{implied} = 20.67\%$.

This would protect us in case the crash of 10 per cent happens on day one from the current levels in the market. Of course it does not protect us from larger moves down, nor if the volatility after this event is elevated. If we think that after such an event the volatility rises to 20 per cent, then we should charge at least 20 per cent of volatility for this option, but we would still need to charge the one-crash event as a premium. The option price with a volatility of 20 per cent is given by the Black–Scholes formula: 47.63. Adding the risk premium on top of this gives a price of 59.91 euro for the 10 per cent OTM put. This related implied volatility is given by 22.59 per cent.

Of course we can make this analysis more precise by trying to time the crash as well. One can for example assume that the option remains within the 18 per cent volatility regime for 10 days and then the crash occurs, after which it enters into the 20 per cent volatility regime. We already showed in Chapter 7 how to calculate the combined volatility. One can then calculate the risk premium based on a similar argument as above (but with a gamma calculated from an option with 10 extra days on the mileage).

How would we adjust the high-strike implied volatility for the OTM call option? Here the argument is similar, but of course there is no crash event that we want to price in. In fact, the reasoning is as follows: if the market keeps trending up, how much would this lower the volatility? Typically the correction on the call-side is smaller, by which we mean that the volatility adjustment is of a smaller order of magnitude. For example, we might ask if the market keeps trending upwards towards the strike level of the currently OTM call, what level of volatility will we have reached? It is an easy exercise to mix the time-dependent model $\sigma(t)$ into the picture and calculate the final implied volatility one would like to charge.

We calculated above that a 'normal' move under an 18 per cent volatility is given by 13.16 euro or 0.88 per cent. Before we reach the strike level of the OTM call, we need to breach 150 euro or roughly 11 such moves. Of course in reality, the gamma and theta will also keep changing as the underlying price changes and time ticks further. If every day corresponds to an up move, and after every such day the actual move reduces to 99 per cent of its predicted move (so the return is set to 99 per cent of the actual return that neutralises the gamma loss versus the original theta), we see in the table below that the profit from hedging after 11 days (or when we reach the strike level) has already accumulated to 0.10. At first sight this might not seem like much, but compared to the theta of 9 cents a day, it is quite substantial.

As a rough approximation, we can calculate the 11 day theta as $11 \cdot \theta_{1d} = -1.05$. If we know that we will make 0.10 extra cents, we can find the volatility parameter that actually gives a theta over 11 days of $-1.05 + 0.10 = -0.96$ or a one day theta of $\theta_{1d} = -0.0869$. The reader can verify with the Black–Scholes theta formula that the implied volatility that corresponds to such a theta is given by $\sigma = 16.90\%$.

Day	$S(t)$	Γ	θ_{1d}	ΔS	$\log(S(t+\Delta t)/S(t))$	99% applied	P&L
1	1500.00	0.001104	−0.0956	13.16	0.87%	1500.00	
2	1513.16	0.001055	−0.0935	13.31	0.88%	1513.03	0.002
3	1526.47	0.001006	−0.0911	13.46	0.88%	1526.17	0.004
4	1539.93	0.000956	−0.0885	13.61	0.88%	1539.46	0.006
5	1553.54	0.000906	−0.0858	13.76	0.88%	1552.91	0.008
6	1567.30	0.000857	−0.0829	13.91	0.88%	1566.50	0.010
7	1581.21	0.000808	−0.0798	14.06	0.89%	1580.24	0.011
8	1595.27	0.000760	−0.0767	14.21	0.89%	1594.13	0.012
9	1609.48	0.000712	−0.0734	14.36	0.89%	1608.18	0.013
10	1623.84	0.000666	−0.0701	14.52	0.89%	1622.37	0.014
11	1638.36	0.000620	−0.0667	14.67	0.89%	1636.72	0.015
12	1653.02						
						Total	0.10

Note that with this implied volatility $\sigma = 16.90\%$ the option price becomes 52.58 euro versus the 60 euro we had started from.

The above arguments provide us with tools on how to use the BS model with extra scenarios to quantify risks and price options. When we generalise this, we could easily see that there are a few parameters that we are using to extend the regular BS price.

1. The jump size: we had fixed it in the above example to a 10 per cent crash but we could easily incorporate any other number.
2. The jump frequency: so far we took into account only one such jump but we don't have to limit ourselves to this. We can take as many jumps as we want.
3. The behaviour after the jump: we assumed that after the jump the volatility was elevated compared to the level before the jump.
4. The jump timing: timing is in fact important, especially when we assume that the volatility changes after the jump.

When extending the above argument, one can easily take a more exotic model such as a jump diffusion model [112, 36]. The jump frequency is typically modelled by a compound Poisson process [133, 74] and the jump size is often modelled with an independent normal distribution. To keep it tractable, one typically assumes independence between the jump and the regular Brownian motion, but one does not have to do this. Regime switching models [20, 21] are very capable of switching between volatility levels. The mathematics in such more advanced models is much more involved and the numerical instabilities in the calibration require a lot of care to resolve.

8.5 Measuring and Trading Skew

In the context of option prices, the skew is the difference in implied volatility between OTM, ATM and ITM options. Usually the skew is observed from the viewpoint of the ATM option. Now that we have established that not only the option price but also the implied volatility depends on the exact strike and maturity of the option, we can write this implied volatility as $\sigma_{imp}(K, T)$ and in fact it is a surface , as the illustration in Figure 8.2 shows.

The skew λ in any point of this surface is defined [64] as the variation of the implied volatility when the strike moves but the expiry or time to maturity is kept fixed:

$$\lambda = \frac{\partial \sigma_{imp}(K, T)}{\partial K}.$$ (8.1)

Of course, within the Black–Scholes model the skew is zero as the model dictates we should use one and the same volatility for all strikes.

Very often one is interested in the skew around the ATM point. Let's use the above example to calculate the skew we came up with ourselves in the previous section. For the sake of simplicity we will assume we didn't touch the ATM volatility, except for the margin we added initially.

S/K	90%	100%	110%
σ_{imp}	22.59%	18.18%	16.90%
π_C	225.36	116.50	52.58
π_P	59.91	97.35	179.73

From these numbers we can then calculate the skew around the ATM point. In fact there are three ways to numerically approximate (8.1) depending on how we discretise this formula. Denote the low strike as K_{low}, the high strike as K_{high} and the ATM strike

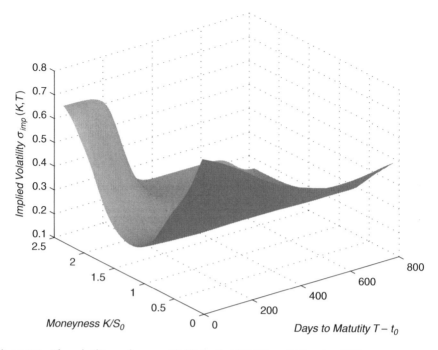

Figure 8.2   The volatility surface $\sigma_{imp}(K, T)$ for the S&P 500 on 19 October 2009.

as K. It is very common to scale out the level of the index itself and just refer to the percentage levels of moneyness for the strike. This makes the skew more standardised. Then the three discretisations become:

$$\lambda = \frac{\sigma_{imp}\left(K_{high}, T\right) - \sigma_{imp}(K, T)}{K_{high} - K} = \frac{16.90\% - 18.18\%}{10\%} = -0.1280 \qquad (8.2)$$

$$\lambda = \frac{\sigma_{imp}(K, T) - \sigma_{imp}(K_{low}, T)}{K - K_{low}} = \frac{18.18\% - 22.59\%}{10\%} = -0.4410 \qquad (8.3)$$

$$\lambda = \frac{\sigma_{imp}\left(K_{high}, T\right) - \sigma_{imp}(K_{low}, T)}{K_{high} - K_{low}} = \frac{16.90\% - 22.59\%}{20\%} = -0.2845. \qquad (8.4)$$

Just like the vega, the industry typically handles a different convention than just the partial derivative. For example, going back to (8.2), we are effectively saying that if the moneyness goes down by 10 per cent (or in other words if we take a 10 per cent higher strike), we have to take our ATM volatility and decrease it by 1.280 per cent. The put-side skew, which is typically larger (more precisely more negative) reads -4.41 per cent and the combined skew reads -2.85 per cent. Depending on the house rules one typically uses 10 per cent OTM or 25 per cent OTM options to define the skew, but this is much more of a convention than a rule.

If we want to use more than one number for the put- and call- side, we can formulate a table with moneyness in one column and the skew number that needs to be added onto the ATM volatility.

Moneyness	Volatility addon or skew
70%	+13.66%
80%	+9.05%
90%	+4.52%
95%	+2.20%
100%	0.00%
105%	−2.03%
110%	−3.82%
120%	−6.57%
130%	−8.77%

(8.5)

One question naturally arises when talking about skew. It is clear by now that skew comes about when we adjust option prices beyond the Black–Scholes model. Can we do this unlimitedly? Can we use any skew shape that we wish? The answer is no. We will continue to work with the above example but we will convert all implied volatilities to put option prices. In the table above, we see that the ATM put option has a price of 97.35. This immediately sets a cap or ceiling on the price for the OTM put option. A 10 per cent OTM put option has to be cheaper than the ATM put option, otherwise there would be a nice arbitrage in the option prices. Translated into implied volatility, this means that the volatility for this strike cannot exceed 30.10 per cent. Any higher implied volatility would mean the OTM put option becomes as expensive as the ATM put.

There are a handful of rules [28, 41, 110] that need to be honoured in pricing options, all of which come about by the non-arbitrage argument.

8.5.1 Option Prices Are Increasing/Decreasing

As pointed out in the above argument, put option prices have to be increasing when you increase the strike. Similarly, call option prices are decreasing with increasing strike:

$$K < K' \Longrightarrow \begin{cases} \pi_C(K,T) \geq \pi_C(K',T) \\ \pi_P(K,T) \leq \pi_P(K',T). \end{cases}$$

(8.6)

What does this signify to a trader? It means Bull call spreads and Bull put spreads have a positive price.

A *bull call spread* is a position where you buy a call option with a lower strike and you sell a call option with a higher strike. The payout of such an option is given in Figure 8.3(*a*). Since the payout is always positive, the premium for such a strategy has to be positive as well (again, otherwise there would be an arbitrage).

A *bull put spread* is a strategy where you buy the put with the lower strike and you sell the put with the higher strike. The payout is of exactly the same form, which can of course be understood from the put–call parity. These strategies are referred to as bull strategies because the payout of such strategies arises when the market rises or in trader's terms when there is a bull market.

Translating this back to the implied volatility, one can see that this means that the skew cannot be too steep. What 'too' steep means depends on all the parameters

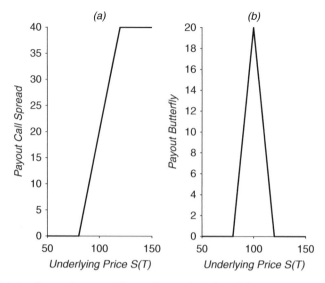

Figure 8.3 (a) A call spread strategy: long a low strike call and short a higher strike call. (b) A butterfly strategy: long a low strike call, long a high strike call and short two calls with a strike in the middle of the low and high. Both strategies have a payout function (intrinsic value) that is always positive.

involved, in particular the time to maturity. Of course for shorter dated options, where the vega is very small, the difference between the implied volatilities across the strikes can be a lot larger before the nominal impact becomes material enough to introduce an arbitrage, so it is not unexpected to see very steep skews for short maturities. This is, of course, a mathematical argument. It is not because it is possible that we should see them, but as we argued earlier, the jump risk on the short-dated options is very large so in normal market circumstances we do see these steep skews, as can be seen in Figure 8.2 or Figure 8.4.

8.5.2 Can We Smile any Which Way We Want?

Another type of arbitrage that can arise is the one where the convexity of the skew curve gets messed up. Let's use the call option prices this time. Assume that we price the ITM call option at 175 euro. We see that the prices are still nicely decreasing with strike, so there is no problem there. However, let's assume that we price the following butterfly strategy: buy one call option with strike 1350, sell two ATM call options and buy one call option with strike 1600. From the payout graph in Figure 8.3(b), we can see that once again this payout is always positive, so the premium for the strategy has to be positive as well. Let us verify: $175 - 2 \cdot 116.50 + 52.58 = -5.42$. That means that we actually get paid to take such a strategy on our books. Great, thank you very much. Collect the arbitrage money and smile some more.

The butterfly rule is a rule across three strikes. When we formulate this mathematically,

$$K < K' < K'' \Longrightarrow \pi_C(K, T) - 2\pi_C(K', T) + \pi_C(K'', T) \geq 0, \qquad (8.7)$$

we can show it is related to the probability density. How do we jump from expression (8.7) to a probability density?

In Section 1.6.3, we mentioned that the underlying distribution function that can be used to find any option price for the Black–Scholes is the lognormal density function. But of course that was before we started changing the prices across the strikes. Recalling expression (1.12), and calculating the second order partial derivative with respect to the strike price K brings us to [152, 125]

$$\frac{\partial^2 \pi_C}{\partial K^2}(\cdot, T) = \exp(-rT) \cdot f(\cdot, T),$$

and of course the discretisation of the partial derivative is exactly the butterfly strategy where f is the density function of the underlying price distribution. Although we initially wrote down this density function as being the lognormal distribution, it can be any density function. In fact, as soon as we start fiddling around with the Black–Scholes model as we are doing now, we are in fact changing the distribution from a lognormal one to something else. The butterfly rule says that is all fine, but we just need to ensure that the density function (or any of its discretisations) remains positive, which is a fair challenge.

All of this is closely related to local volatility models first introduced by Dupire [56, 57]. We won't go into any further detail, but we hope the reader can appreciate that these kinds of boundaries as to how we can choose our option prices (and implied volatilities) make sense. It is common practice to set the skew in a similar way as we did above: define the option price or the implied volatility for a fixed set of strikes. Interpolation techniques [54, 62] are then used to come up with the implied volatility for other strikes, both inside and outside of this range. However, in the wings, this typically leads to arbitrage, for which we now have a set of rules to check.

8.5.3 Implied Distribution and Probabilities

Once we have a density function $f(\cdot)$ for the underlying price process $S(t)$, we can not only calculate prices of European call and put options as we explained in Section 1.6.3, but in fact we can calculate all desired statistical properties of the stock price $S(t)$. One obvious question one could ask is what is the probability that the stock price will be below a certain level K at a certain time T:

$$\Pr(S(T) < K).$$

Since we know the probability distribution that is implied by the options market, we can then calculate

$$\Pr(S(T) < K) = \int_0^K f(s)\,ds.$$

And this is exactly where one has to be careful. The distributions that are implied by the option prices are so-called risk-neutral probability distributions [152, 125]. In Chapter 1 we argued for both the binomial tree model and the Black–Scholes model that the drift or direction was not relevant for hedging the options and as a consequence had no influence on the price. It was merely the cost of hedging that determined the price and cost of hedging was related to the volatility. In this chapter we extended the BS model to take into account extra risk premiums and saw how this gets reflected in the implied volatility.

Option prices have been adjusted because of the volatility behaviour, the skew and the fat tails of the distribution of returns. Admittedly one could argue that the skew biases the direction of the stock, but it is still not a drift term. This means that one cannot expect to have any knowledge of the probability that the stock price will be below a certain threshold. There is a mathematical difference between the risk-neutral probabilities and the real world or historical probabilities and, unfortunately, over longer periods of observation the drift term becomes important for calculating such probabilities.

For example, in (1.8) or (1.9) we can see that the drift term is of the form $\mu \cdot (t - t_0)$ and the volatility term is of the form $\sigma \sqrt{t - t_0}$. This implies that when looking at small timesteps the volatility term is more important as $\Delta t < \sqrt{\Delta t}$, but for larger timesteps the drift term cannot be ignored. Of course the rebalancing of the hedging is done frequently and therefore the drift does not enter into the picture.

8.6 Parametric Skew Model

More exotic models such as Heston [81] or any Lévy model [133] have skew baked into the model directly. These kinds of models operate from a larger set of parameters and, although typically each parameter has a stronger effect than others on one of the market features such as ATM volatility, the skew or the convexity, there are always cross effects that make it harder to isolate the effects and use these models on an intuitive basis when compared to the Black–Scholes model.

This is why using the Black–Scholes model is still so relevant. Throughout the book, we have layered up the complexity, and even when introducing skew we kept formulating our thoughts in terms of the Black–Scholes prices and Greeks. That's the true beauty of the model. Even when breaking it, we can continue using it. It provides a framework that can be stretched beyond its boundaries and still remain powerful.

A lot of proposals have been formulated to interpolate and extrapolate the implied volatility surface given a few points [62]. As we mentioned above, near-expiry options typically have a stronger skew. We already mentioned that this is partly due to the low vega effect. The other reason that amplifies the skew in short-dated options is that the jump risk becomes more material. Remember that the gamma blows out near expiry and the crash risk we talked about earlier can have a stronger impact. Because of this risk, one typically sees a stronger skew in near-expiry options compared to long-dated options.

A very simple parametric representation with just one parameter is given by

$$\sigma(K, T) = \sigma_{ATM}(T) + \gamma \frac{\log K/S}{\sqrt{T - t_0}}. \tag{8.8}$$

Unfortunately this formula is not rich enough to capture all the skew shapes.

Table (8.5) had 73 days before expiry. Try to fit the parameter γ to this data. This dataset lends itself to this parametric model (make a scatter plot $(\log(S/K), \sigma(K) - \sigma_{ATM})$ to understand why). Try to do the same with the examples (8.2), (8.3), (8.4) and explain why the model does not work.

An multi-parameter extension of this parametric form is the parabolic skew function

$$\sigma(K, T) = \sigma_{ATM}(T) + \gamma_1 \frac{\log K/S}{\sqrt{T - t_0}} + \gamma_2 \left(\frac{\log K/S}{\sqrt{T - t_0}}\right)^2. \qquad (8.9)$$

Obviously parabolic shapes blow up in the wings and these models are known to contain arbitrage quite quickly, but because of the easy intuition they are still used. The interested reader is referred to Jim Gatheral's SVI [64] that uses a parametric formulation in variance rather than in volatility, and it is easier to keep the arbitrage out of that model:

$$\sigma(K, T) = \sqrt{a + b\left\{\rho\left(\log K - m\right) + \sqrt{\left(\log K - m\right)^2 + \sigma^2}\right\}}, \qquad (8.10)$$

where fits are done per maturity and as a consequence all parameters are dependent on the maturity.

8.7 The Skews in the Market Across Maturities

Now that we understand what skew is, how it arises and where its limitations are, it's time to have a look at various skew and smile shapes in Figure 8.4. There are a few generic observations we can make. First of all, we see that for short-dated options the skew is sharper. This means there is more skew. We already commented above that the vega is small, and as a consequence small deviations from the option price lead to larger shifts in the implied volatility.

This is not, however, how a trader will justify the sharper skew near maturity. He will argue that near maturity the gamma risk is much larger. If things move, it will be for the remainder of the lifetime (as there is not much time left before expiry), whereas for longer-dated options, such a spike will normalise back and hence the overall risk is smaller. The jump risk for near expiry options is much larger. The most extreme example is probably the option that is 1 per cent OTM but will expire in one day. There is still a good chance it will expire ITM and the typical volatility will not capture this spike risk.

Another observation we can make is that the volatility will flatten out in the wings. We can already see this in Figure 8.4 on the put-side. If we kept extrapolating the skew in the wings, we would get ourselves into an arbitrage again. It can be shown [108, 14] that volatility cannot keep rising linearly (see the next section). One has to be careful

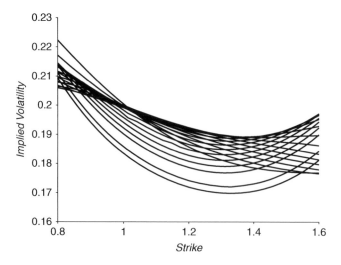

Figure 8.4   A wide variety of skew functions $K \to \sigma_{imp}(K, T)$ across a variety of maturities ranging from six months to five years.

with some standard models that are usually very effective for options that are being traded. Those traded options are usually not that far in the wings. But once an option is executed it can remain on the books for years. During that time, the market can move substantially and these old options can be really far ITM or OTM. Using a standard extrapolation model can lead to an arbitrage on the valuation. Even parametric models such as (8.8) and (8.9) both suffer from this problem quite severely.

8.8 Non-Arbitrage Conditions

In Sections 7.3 and 8.5 we established relationships that, if not met, could lead to an arbitrage. Given a discrete set of options with various strikes $K_1, K_2, \ldots, K_M$ and maturities $T_1, \ldots, T_N$, it can be shown [28, 110] that if all calendar spreads (see (7.8)), all vertical spreads (see (8.6)) and all butterflies (see (8.7)) are priced positively, the grid of option prices is free of arbitrage.

This means that the verification of arbitrage can be done on a pairwise basis for the spreads and per three for the butterfly. There is no need to investigate the full universe in its entirety. These conditions are formulated in terms of the original option prices. It turns out to be a lot harder to formulate simple rules for the implied volatility function to be without arbitrage. There are some results that limit the behaviour, such as Roger Lee's moment formula [108], which states that for a maturity T, the implied variance

$$\left(\sigma_{imp}(K, T)\right)^2 \sim \log K, \text{ as } K \to 0, \infty$$

behaves as $\log K$ in the wings.

8.9 How Does Skew Change Over Time?

In Chapter 7 we elaborated on how volatility can change over time. As a consequence we know there is volatility term structure. In this chapter we focused on the strike dependency of the implied volatility. Naturally, the next question arises: If the market moves around, how does this volatility skew move [32, 125]? Of course there is a substantial amount of randomness in these moves which traders will take positions on, and they will try to monetise this risk by trading. But there is more to say. Before we say more, let's ask this paradoxical question: Once we sell an ATM call option with a given implied volatility, if the market moves away a few percentage points and this call option becomes OTM, will its implied volatility decrease, because that's what the skew tells you? Or will it carry its volatility value for longer, indicating that the skew curve is shifting?

The difference between those two concepts is what market participants describe as sticky strike and sticky delta. Which one is prevailing depends on the market and also on the market conditions. Let's dig a little bit deeper into this.

The *sticky strike rule* is the rule that the volatility sticks to the actual strike level. So if we plotted the skew as a percentage of strike rather than actual strike levels, the curve would shift left or right if the market moved down or up. In this case it makes more sense to plot and use the skew as a function of the exact strikes. Note that parametric formulas are a bit trickier. They can be adjusted to use $S(t_0)$ at the moment of calibration, rather than the current market.

This rule is often attributed to the equity markets and in fact, although most of the exotic option models such as Heston are not adapted for this rule, people have made adjustments to these models to accommodate for it. If options stick to their volatility, then delta hedging these options can be done by sticking to this volatility. The hedging and pricing volatility are then identical and (relatively) stable.

The *sticky delta rule* , however, states that it is the moneyness that determines the level of implied volatility. This means that if we plot the skew as a function of the percentage moneyness (or equivalently as the delta), the plot is unchanged, but if we plot it as a function of the actual strike, the skew curve starts drifting. This rule is typically valid when markets trend but the overall volatility of the market does not change. Foreign exchange markets are typically more of the sticky delta type.

Here the hedging is different. It is quite obvious that if $\sigma_{imp}(K, T) = \sigma_{imp}(K/S, T)$ depends on the moneyness, when the stock value moves by ΔS, we know that the moneyness changes, hence the volatility will change and this will result in a vega term in the delta, similarly to how we had a vega term in the theta in the time-dependent volatility model. The skew-adjusted delta or effective delta is then given by

$$\Delta_{eff} = \Delta - \lambda \cdot \nu.$$

Of course, in no market are the rules this simple and it is typically a bit of a mix of these rules [96, 153, 125] that depicts the real story. And on top of this, nothing lives forever, so in the same way as the level of volatility in the market changes, so does the shape of the skew. All is random, all is uncertain, ready and waiting to be traded.

Bibliography

[1] F. Abergel. *Model calibration for financial derivatives from hedging to pricing.* John Wiley & Sons Inc, 2014.

[2] H. Ahn, M. Dayal, E. Grannan, and G. Swindle. Option replication with transaction costs: General diffusion limits. *The Annals of Applied Probability,* 8(3):pp. 676–707, 1998.

[3] H. Albrecher, P. Mayer, W. Schoutens, and J. Tistaert. The little Heston trap. *Wilmott,* January:pp. 83–92, 2007.

[4] K. I. Amin and J. Bodurtha, James N. Discrete-time valuation of american options with stochastic interest rates. *The Review of Financial Studies,* 8(1):pp. 193–234, 1995.

[5] L. Andersen and J. Andreasen. Static barriers. *Risk Magazine,* September:pp. 120–122, 2000.

[6] T. G. Andersen, T. Bollerslev, F. X. Diebold, and P. Labys. Modeling and forecasting realized volatility. *Econometrica,* 71(2):pp. 579–625, 2003.

[7] G. B. Arfken and H. Weber. *Mathematical methods for physicists.* Elsevier, Boston, 2005.

[8] E. Ayache. What is implied by implied volatility? *Wilmott,* December:pp. 28–35, 2005.

[9] A. H. Aziz, M. Bersani, F. Fauceglia, M. Ikeda, H. Letrï£¡guilly, B. McCormack, B. W. Reynolds, A. Ruff, and A. Seem. Global clampdown on short selling: an overview. *Shearman & Sterling LLP,* 2010.

[10] K. Back. *A course in derivative securities introduction to theory and computation.* Springer, Berlin; New York, 2005.

[11] O. E. Barndorff-Nielsen and N. Shephard. Econometric analysis of realized volatility and its use in estimating stochastic volatility models. *Journal of the Royal Statistical Society. Series B (Statistical Methodology),* 64(2):pp. 253–280, 2002.

[12] S. Basak and G. Chabakauri. Dynamic hedging in incomplete markets: A simple solution. *The Review of Financial Studies,* 25(6):pp. 1845–1896, 2012.

[13] M. Baxter and A. Rennie. *Financial calculus: an introduction to derivative pricing.* Cambridge University Press, Cambridge; New York, NY, 1997.

[14] S. Benaim, P. Friz, and R. Lee. On the black-scholes implied volatility at extreme strikes. 2008.

[15] S. Bianco, F. Corsi, R. Reno, and H. E. Stanley. Intraday lebaron effects. *Proceedings of the National Academy of Sciences of the United States of America,* 106(28):pp. 11439–11443, 2009.

[16] N. H. Bingham and R. Kiesel. *Risk-neutral valuation: pricing and hedging of financial derivatives.* Springer, Sheffield, UK; New York, 2004.

[17] T. Björk. *Arbitrage theory in continuous time.* Oxford University Press, Oxford; New York, 2004.

[18] F. Black and M. Scholes. The pricing of options and corporate liabilities. *Journal of Political Economy,* 81(3):pp. 637–654, 1973.

[19] P. Boyle and D. Emanuel. Discretely adjusted option hedges. *Journal of financial Economics,* 8:pp. 259–282, 1980.

[20] D. Brigo and F. Mercurio. Implied volatility: A mixed up smile. *Risk Magazine,* September:pp. 123–126, 2000.

[21] D. Brigo and F. Mercurio. Lognormal-mixture dynamics and calibration to market volatility smiles. *International Journal of Theoretical and Applied Finance,* 5(4):pp. 427–446, 2002.

[22] D. Brigo and F. Mercurio. *Interest rate models: Theory and practice.* Springer, Berlin; New York, 2007.

[23] D. C. Brody, L. P. Hughston, and E. Mackie. General theory of geometric levy models for dynamic asset pricing. *Proceedings: Mathematical, Physical and Engineering Sciences,* 468(2142):pp. 1778–1798, 2012.

[24] H. Buehler. *Volatility markets consistent modeling, hedging, and practical implementation of variance swap market models.* VDM Verlag Dr. Müller, Saarbrücken, 2009.

[25] J. Y. Campbell, S. J. Grossman, and J. Wang. Trading volume and serial correlation in stock returns. *The Quarterly Journal of Economics*, 108(4):pp. 905–939, 1993.

[26] P. Carr and J. Bowie. Static simplicity. *Risk Magazine*, August:pp. 44–50, 1994.

[27] P. Carr and D. Madan. Option valuation using the fast fourier transform. *Journal of Computational Finance*, 2:pp. 61–73, 1998.

[28] P. Carr and D. Madan. A note on sufficient conditions for no arbitrage. *Finance Research Letters*, 2:pp. 125–130, 2005.

[29] U. Cetin, R. Jarrow, P. Protter, and M. Warachka. Pricing options in an extended black scholes economy with illiquidity: Theory and empirical evidence. *The Review of Financial Studies*, 19(2):pp. 493–529, 2006.

[30] C. W. Chang and J. S. K. Chang. Option pricing with stochastic volatility: Information-time vs. calendar-time. *Management Science*, 42(7):pp. 974–991, 1996.

[31] A. Chisholm. *Derivatives demystified a step-by-step guide to forwards, futures, swaps and options*. Wiley, Hoboken, 2010.

[32] P. Christoffersen, S. Heston, and K. Jacobs. The shape and term structure of the index option smirk: Why multifactor stochastic volatility models work so well. *Management Science*, 55(12): pp. 1914–1932, 2009.

[33] I. J. Clark. *Foreign exchange option pricing: a practitioner's guide*. Wiley, Chichester, West Sussex, UK, 2011.

[34] I. J. Clark. *Commodity option pricing: a practitioner's guide*. Wiley, Chichester, West Sussex, UK, 2014.

[35] R. Cont. Empirical properties of asset returns: stylized facts and statistical issues. *Quantitative Finance*, 1:pp. 223–236, 2001.

[36] R. Cont and P. Tankov. *Financial modelling with jump processes*. Chapman & Hall/CRC, Boca Raton, Fla., 2004.

[37] R. Cooper. *Corporate treasury and cash management*. Palgrave Macmillan, Houndmills, 2004.

[38] J. Corcuera, F. Guillaume, D. Madan, and W. Schoutens. Implied liquidity: Towards stochastic liquidity modelling and liquidity trading. *International Journal of Portfolio Analysis and Management*, 1(1):pp. 80–91, 2012.

[39] J. M. Corcuera, F. Guillaume, P. Leoni, and W. Schoutens. Implied levy volatility. *Quantitative Finance*, 9(4):pp. 383–393, 2009.

[40] J. C. Cox, S. A. Ross, and M. Rubinstein. Option pricing: A simplified approach. *Journal of Financial Economics*, 7(3):pp. 229, 1979.

[41] J. C. Cox and M. Rubinstein. *Options markets*. Prentice-Hall, Englewood Cliffs, NJ, 1985.

[42] M. Cummins, F. Murphy, and J. J. H. Miller. *Topics in numerical methods for finance.* Springer, New York, 2012.

[43] G. Da Prato. *Kolmogorov equations for stochastic PDEs*. Birkhäuser Verlag, Basel; Boston, 2004.

[44] J. de Spiegeleer and W. Schoutens. *The handbook of convertible bonds: pricing, strategies and risk management*. Wiley; John Wiley [distributor], Hoboken, NJ; Chichester, 2011.

[45] J. de Spiegeleer, C. van Hulle, and W. Schoutens. *Handbook of hybrid securities: strategies, pricing and risk management*. John Wiley, Hoboken, 2014.

[46] G. Deelstra, G. Plantin, U. Ray, and G. Deelstra. *Risk theory and reinsurance*. Springer-Verlag, London, 2014.

[47] E. Derman. *Models behaving badly: why confusing illusion with reality can lead to disaster, on Wall Street and in life*. Free Press, New York, 2012.

[48] E. Derman, D. Ergener, and I. Kani. Static options replication. *Journal of Derivatives*, 2(4): pp. 78–95, 1995.

[49] J. Detemple. *American-style derivatives: valuation and computation*. Taylor & Francis, Boca Raton [Fla.], 2006.

[50] J. N. Dewynne, A. E. Whalley, and P. Wilmott. Path-dependent options and transaction costs. *Philosophical Transactions: Physical Sciences and Engineering*, 347(1684):pp. 517–529, 1994.

[51] R. W. Dimand. The case of brownian motion: A note on bachelier's contribution. *The British Journal for the History of Science*, 26(2):pp. 233–234, 1993.

[52] D. A. Dubofsky and T. W. Miller. *Derivatives: valuation and risk management*. Oxford Univ. Press, New York, NY, 2003.

[53] M. J. Dueker. Markov switching in garch processes and mean-reverting stock-market volatility. *Journal of Business & Economic Statistics*, 15(1):pp. 26–34, 1997.

[54] B. Dumas, J. Fleming, and R. E. Whaley. Implied volatility functions: Empirical tests. *The Journal of Finance*, 53(6):pp. 2059–2106, 1998.

[55] N. Dunbar. *The devil's derivatives: the untold story of the slick traders and hapless regulators who almost blew up Wall Street–and are ready to do it again.* Harvard Business Review Press, Boston, Mass., 2011.

[56] B. Dupire. Pricing and hedging with smiles. *Proceedings AFFI Conf, La Baule*, June, 1993.

[57] B. Dupire. Pricing with a smile. *Risk Magazine*, 7(1):pp. 18–20, 1994.

[58] B. A. Eales and M. Choudhry. *Derivative instruments a guide to theory and practice.* Butterworth-Heinemann, Oxford; Boston, 2003.

[59] E. Eberlein and U. Keller. Hyperbolic distributions in finance. *Bernoulli*, 1(3):pp. 281–299, 1995.

[60] L. H. Ederington and W. Guan. Higher order greeks. *The Journal of Derivatives*, 14(3):pp. 7–34, 2007.

[61] L. C. Evans. *An introduction to stochastic differential equations.* American Mathematical Society, 2013.

[62] M. R. Fengler. *Semiparametric modeling of implied volatility.* Springer, Berlin; New York, 2005.

[63] J. P. Fouque, G. Papanicolaou, R. Sircar, and K. Solna. Singular perturbations in option pricing. *SIAM Journal on Applied Mathematics*, 63(5):pp. 1648–1665, 2003.

[64] J. Gatheral. *The volatility surface: a practitioner's guide.* John Wiley & Sons, Hoboken, NJ, 2006.

[65] H. Geman. *Commodities and commodity derivatives: modelling and pricing for agriculturals, metals, and energy.* John Wiley & Sons, West Sussex, 2005.

[66] T. J. George and F. A. Longstaff. Bid-ask spreads and trading activity in the s&p 100 index options market. *The Journal of Financial and Quantitative Analysis*, 28(3):pp. 381–397, 1993.

[67] H. U. Gerber and V. S. Versicherungsmathematiker. *Life insurance mathematics.* Springer, Berlin; New York, 1997.

[68] R. Geske. The pricing of options with stochastic dividend yield. *The Journal of Finance*, 33(2):pp. 617–625, 1978.

[69] D. T. Gillespie and E. Seitaridou. *Simple Brownian diffusion: an introduction to the standard theoretical models.* OUP, Oxford, 2013.

[70] P. Glasserman. *Monte Carlo methods in financial engineering.* Springer, New York, 2003.

[71] L. Y. Goh and D. Allen. A note on put–call parity and the market efficiency of the London traded options market. *Managerial and Decision Economics*, 5(2):pp. 85–90, 1984.

[72] P. Grandits. Frequent hedging under transaction costs and a nonlinear Fokker-Planck pde. *SIAM Journal on Applied Mathematics*, 62(2):pp. 541–562, 2001.

[73] F. Guillaume and W. Schoutens. Heston model: The variance swap calibration. *Journal of Optimization Theory and Applications*, pages pp. 1–14, 2013.

[74] A. K. Gupta, W. Zeng, and Y. Wu. *Probability and statistical models: Foundations for problems in reliability and financial mathematics.* Springer Science+Business Media, LLC, Boston, 2010.

[75] J. Guyon and P. Henry-Labordere. *Nonlinear option pricing.* Financial Mathematics Series. Chapman and Hall/CRC, 2013.

[76] W. Hafner and H. Zimmermann. *Vinzenz Bronzin's option pricing models exposition and appraisal.* Springer, Berlin; London, 2009.

[77] E. G. Haug. The options genius. *Wilmott*, July, 2001.

[78] E. G. Haug. *The complete guide to option pricing formulas.* McGraw-Hill, New York, 2007.

[79] E. G. Haug. *Derivatives: models on models.* John Wiley, Chichester, 2007.

[80] S. A. Heffernan. *Modern banking in theory and practice.* Wiley, Chichester, England; New York, N.Y., 1996.

[81] S. L. Heston. A closed form solution for options with stochastic volatility with applications to bond and currency options. *Review of Financial Studies*, 6:pp. 327–343, 1993.

[82] S. L. Heston, R. A. Korajczyk, and R. Sadka. Intraday patterns in the cross-section of stock returns. *The Journal of Finance*, 65(4):pp. 1369–1407, 2010.

[83] R. Heynen, A. Kemna, and T. Vorst. Analysis of the term structure of implied volatilities. *The Journal of Financial and Quantitative Analysis*, 29(1):pp. 31–56, 1994.

[84] A. Hirsa. *Computational methods in finance.* CRC Press, Boca Raton, FL, 2013.

[85] T. S. Ho, R. C. Stapleton, and M. G. Subrahmanyam. The valuation of American options with stochastic interest rates: A generalization of the Geske-Johnson technique. *The Journal of Finance*, 52(2):pp. 827–840, 1997.

[86] D. Hobson. Robust hedging of the lookback option. *Finance and Stochastics*, 2:pp. 329–347, 1998.

[87] T. Hoggard, A. E. Whalley, and Wi. Heding option portfolios in the presence of transaction costs. *Advances in Futures and Options Research*, 7:pp. 21–35, 1994.

[88] Y. C. Huang and S. H. Chan. Trading behavior on expiration days and quarter-end days: The effect of a new closing method. *Emerging Markets Finance & Trade*, 46(4):pp. 105–125, 2010.

[89] J. Hull. *Options, futures, and other derivatives*. Pearson Eduation Limited and Associated Companies throughout the world, Essex, England, 2012.

[90] J. Hull and A. White. CVA and wrong way risk. *Financial Analysts Journal*, 68(5):pp. 58–69, 2012.

[91] J. Hull and A. White. The FVA debate. *Risk Magazine*, 25th Anniversary(7):pp. 83–85, 2012.

[92] J. Hull and A. White. Libor vs. OIS. *Journal of Investment Management*, 11(3):pp. 14–27, 2013.

[93] P. Jäckel. *Monte Carlo methods in finance*. J. Wiley, Chichester, West Sussex, England, 2002.

[94] A. Javaheri. *Inside volatility arbitrage: the secrets of skewness*. John Wiley, Hoboken, NJ, 2005.

[95] M. S. Joshi. *C++ design patterns and derivatives pricing*. Cambridge University Press, Cambridge, UK ; New York, 2008.

[96] M. S. Joshi. *The concepts and practice of mathematical finance*. Cambridge University Press, Cambridge; New York, 2008.

[97] C. Kahl and P. Jaeckel. Not-so-complex logarithms in the Heston model. *Wilmott*, September:pp. 94–103, 2005.

[98] J. Kallsen and A. Pauwels. Variance-optimal hedging in general affine stochastic volatility models. *Advances in Applied Probability*, 42(1):pp. 83–105, 2010.

[99] A. Kamara and T. W. Miller Jr. Daily and intradaily tests of european put-call parity. *The Journal of Financial and Quantitative Analysis*, 30(4):pp. 519–539, 1995.

[100] I. Karatzas and S. E. Shreve. *Brownian motion and stochastic calculus*. Springer, New York, 1998.

[101] J. S. Kennedy, P. A. Forsyth, and K. R. Vetzal. Dynamic hedging under jump diffusion with transaction costs. *Operations Research*, 57(3):pp. 541–559, 2009.

[102] R. C. Klemkosky and B. G. Resnick. Put-call parity and market efficiency. *The Journal of Finance*, 34(5):pp. 1141–1155, 1979.

[103] M. Kline. *Calculus: an intuitive and physical approach*. Dover, Mineola (NY), 1998.

[104] P. E. Kloeden and E. Platen. *Numerical solution of stochastic differential equations*. Springer, Berlin, 2010.

[105] A. N. Kolmogorov. *Foundations of the Theory of Probability*. Martino Fine Books, Nov. 2013.

[106] P. E. Kopp. *Probability for finance*. Cambridge University Press, Cambridge, 2013.

[107] G. F. Lawler. *Random walk and the heat equation*. American Mathematical Society, Providence, R.I., 2010.

[108] R. Lee. The moment formula for implied volatility at extreme strikes. *Mathematical Finance*, 14(4):pp. 469–480, 2004.

[109] H. E. Leland. Option pricing and replication with transation costs. *Journal of Finance*, 40:pp. 1283–1301, 1985.

[110] F. Mercurio. No-arbitrage conditions for a finite options system.

[111] F. Mercurio and T. Vorst. Option pricing with hedging at fixed trading dates. *Applied Mathematical Finance*, 3:pp. 135–158, 1996.

[112] R. Merton. Option pricing when underlying stock returns are discontinuous. *Journal of Financial Economics*, 3:pp. 125–144, 1976.

[113] R. C. Merton. Theory of rational option pricing. *The Bell Journal of Economics and Management Science*, 4(1):pp. 141–183, 1973.

[114] R. C. Merton. Paul Samuelson and financial economics. *The American Economist*, 50(2):pp. 9–31, 2006.

[115] T. Mikosch. *Elementary stochastic calculus with finance in view*. World Scientific Publ., Singapore; River Edge, NJ, 1998.

[116] T. Mikosch. *Non-Life Insurance Mathematics: An Introduction with the Poisson Process*. Springer-Verlag Berlin Heidelberg, Berlin, Heidelberg, 2009.

[117] M. H. Miller. *Merton Miller on Derivatives*. Wiley, New York, 1997.

[118] S. Natenberg. *Option volatility and pricing: advanced trading strategies and techniques*. McGraw-Hill, New York [etc.], 1994.

[119] S. Natenberg. *Basic option volatility strategies: understanding popular pricing models*. Marketplace Books, Glenelg, MD, 2009.

[120] B. K. Øksendal. *Stochastic differential equations: an introduction with applications.* Springer, Berlin; New York, 2003.

[121] A. Olivieri and E. Pitacco. *Introduction to insurance mathematics technical and financial features of risk transfers.* Springer, Berlin, 2011.

[122] A. Pelsser. *Efficient methods for valuing interest rate derivatives.* Springer London, London, 2000.

[123] S. R. Pliska. *Introduction to mathematical finance: discrete time models.* Blackwell Publishers, Malden, Mass., 1998.

[124] R. Rebonato. *Modern pricing of interest-rate derivatives: the LIBOR market model and beyond.* Princeton University Press, Princeton, NJ, 2002.

[125] R. Rebonato. *Volatility and correlation.* Wiley, Chichester, 2004.

[126] D. Revuz and M. Yor. *Continuous martingales and Brownian motion.* Springer, Berlin; New York, 2005.

[127] R. Rhoads. *Trading VIX derivatives trading and hedging strategies using VIX futures, options, and exchange-traded notes.* Wiley, Hoboken, NJ, 2011.

[128] P. Richter. Seven days' trading make one weak? the Sunday trading issue as an index of secularization. *The British Journal of Sociology,* 45(3):pp. 333–348, 1994.

[129] S. Ross. *A first course in probability.* Pearson, 2014.

[130] V. I. Rotar. *Actuarial models: the mathematics of insurance.* Chapman & Hall/CRC, Boca Raton, FL, 2007.

[131] M. Rubinstein. Implied binomial trees. *The Journal of Finance,* 49(3):pp. 771–818, 1994.

[132] W. Rudin. *Principles of mathematical analysis.* McGraw-Hill, New York, 1976.

[133] W. Schoutens. *Lévy processes in finance: pricing financial derivatives.* Wiley, West Sussex, 2003.

[134] W. Schoutens and J. Cariboni. *Lévy processes in credit risk.* John Wiley & Sons, Chichester, UK, 2009.

[135] S. E. Shreve. *Stochastic calculus for finance 2, 2,.* Springer, New York, NY; Heidelberg, 2004.

[136] S. E. Shreve. *Stochastic calculus for finance.* Springer, New York, 2005.

[137] J. Shu and J. Zhang. The relationship between implied and realized volatility of S&P500 index. *Wilmott,* January, 2003.

[138] M. Spivak. *Calculus.* Cambridge University Press, Cambridge, 2006.

[139] E. J. Sullivan and T. M. Weithers. Louis bachelier: The father of modern option pricing theory. *The Journal of Economic Education,* 22(2):pp. 165–171, 1991.

[140] G. Szpiro. *Pricing the future finance, physics, and the 300-year journey to the Black-Scholes equation: a story of genius and discovery.* Basic Books, New York, 2011.

[141] N. Taleb. *Dynamic hedging: Managing vanilla and exotic options.* Wiley, New York (NY), 1997.

[142] K. Toft and C. Xuan. How well can barrier options be hedged by a static portfolio of standard options? *The Journal of Financial Engineering,* 7(2):pp. 147–175, 1998.

[143] K. B. Toft. On the mean-variance tradeoff in option replication with transactions costs. *The Journal of Financial and Quantitative Analysis,* 31(2):pp. 233–263, 1996.

[144] P. Triana. *Lecturing birds on flying: can mathematical theories destroy the financial markets?* John Wiley & Sons, Hoboken, NJ, 2009.

[145] A. L. Turner and E. J. Weigel. Daily stock market volatility: 1928–1989. *Management Science,* 38(11):pp. 1586–1609, 1992.

[146] A. E. Whalley and P. Wilmott. Counting the costs. *Risk Magazine,* 6(10):pp. 59–66, 1993.

[147] U. F. Wiersema. *Brownian motion calculus.* John Wiley & Sons, Chichester; Hoboken, NJ, 2008.

[148] P. Wilmott. Discrete charms. *Risk Magazine,* 7(3):pp. 48–51, 1994.

[149] P. Wilmott. The use, misuse and abuse of mathematics in finance. *Philosophical Transactions: Mathematical, Physical and Engineering Sciences,* 358(1765):pp. 63–73, 2000.

[150] P. Wilmott, editor. *The best of Wilmott. incorporating the quantitative finance review Volume 1.* John Wiley & Sons, Chichester; [Hoboken, NJ], 2005.

[151] P. Wilmott. *The best of Wilmott Volume 2.* Wiley, Hoboken, NJ, 2006.

[152] P. Wilmott. *Paul Wilmott on quantitative finance.* John Wiley & Sons, Chichester, England; Hoboken, NJ, 2006.

[153] P. Wilmott. *Frequently asked questions in quantitative finance including key models, important formulæ, popular contracts, essays and opinions, a history of quantitative finance, sundry lists, the commonest mistakes in quant finance, brainteasers, plenty of straight-talking, the Modellers' Manifesto and lots more.* Wiley, Chichester, UK, 2009.

[154] Y. Zhu, X. Wu, and I. Chern. *Derivative securities and difference methods.* Springer, New York, 2013.

Index

Printed in Great Britain
by Amazon

63619431R00086